The New Prophets
of Capital

The Jacobin series features short interrogations of politics, economics, and culture from a socialist perspective, as an avenue to radical political practice. The books offer critical analysis and engagement with the history and ideas of the Left in an accessible format.

The series is a collaboration between Verso Books and *Jacobin* magazine, which is published quarterly in print and online at jacobinmag.com.

Other titles in this series available from Verso Books:

Playing the Whore by Melissa Gira Grant
Utopia or Bust by Benjamin Kunkel
Strike for America by Micah Uetricht

The New Prophets of Capital

by
NICOLE ASCHOFF

VERSO
London • New York

For Ila and Simi

First published by Verso 2015
© Nicole Aschoff 2015

1 3 5 7 9 10 8 6 4 2

Verso
UK: 6 Meard Street, London W1F 0EG
US: 20 Jay Street, Suite 1010, Brooklyn, NY 11201
www.versobooks.com

Verso is the imprint of New Left Books

ISBN-13: 978-1-78168-810-6 (PB)
eISBN-13: 978-1-78168-811-3 (US)
eISBN-13: 978-1-78168-812-0 (UK)

British Library Cataloguing in Publication Data
A catalogue record for this book is available from the British Library

Library of Congress Cataloging-in-Publication Data
A catalog record for this book is available from the Library of Congress

Typeset in Fournier MT by Hewer Text UK Ltd, Edinburgh
Printed in the US by Maple Press

Contents

Introduction: Storytelling

We are all storytellers. We embellish, ignore, and cherry-pick moments of our lives to create an emergent story of us. The stories we tell are integral to our lives. They help us find friends and lovers, they demonstrate our values and beliefs, they showcase our competence and trustworthiness, and they teach our children how to navigate the world. Our stories make us appear interesting, compassionate, heroic, and responsible. Most of our stories lack potency, though—they linger close to us and get lost in the cacophony of other people's stories. But on rare occasions stories grow, often in direct proportion to the power of their teller, to become big, all-encompassing stories that define a people, a social movement, or a moment in history.

Stories become powerful and defining because people love stories and society needs stories. Big stories reproduce the social order by providing meaning and mooring. They get us out of bed in the morning and remind us where we are going in life. They identify our friends and our enemies. They stir our hopes and allay our fears. They keep alienation at bay.

The big stories we hear and tell today—stories about freedom and terrorists and the American Dream—are as integral to society as the old stories of Anansi, Manas, Beowolf, and Parvati were to the societies that created them.

Capitalist society is particularly in need of stories. Our everyday lives are defined by going to school and to work, caring for our kids, listening to gossip, having a laugh, and stressing about this or that. Yet all of these micro-interactions take place within a set of larger structures and relationships whose primary purpose is to make a profit. The vast majority of people go to jobs that were not created to meet human needs but to give the owners of capital a return on their investment. All of us, wage-earners and capitalists alike, are locked into a system designed to perpetually accumulate more and more profit, not to satisfy human needs or provide for the common good. This is a strange way of organizing society. It goes against our nature as social, mutualistic beings. Yet for capitalism to survive and thrive, people must willingly participate in and reproduce its structures and norms. Coercion and duress work to integrate the poorest and most desperate members of society, but they are not sufficient to ensure the generation of profits in the long term. Large swathes of the population must actively, or at least passively, believe that capitalist society is worth their creativity, energy, and passion, that it will provide a sense of meaning, that it meets their need for justice and security.

But there is nothing intrinsic to the logic of profit-making itself that is capable of providing this sense of meaning and justice. Capitalism must draw upon cultural ideas that exist outside circuits of profit-making, some of which support the norms and structures of capitalism and some of which are critical of capitalism. As sociologists Luc Boltanski and Eva Chiapello argue, capital needs both types: while individual capitalists may attempt to repress and displace challenges to the primacy of profit-making, at the systemic level critical voices are productive and fruitful for capitalism, forcing capitalism to evolve and temporarily resolve some of its contradictions and thus preserving it as a system for the long haul. Indeed, capital's ability to periodically present a new set of legitimating principles that facilitate the willing participation of society accounts for its remarkable longevity despite periodic bouts of deep crisis. Following Max Weber, one of the foremost social thinkers of the twentieth century, Boltanski and Chiapello call this belief system, which justifies and legitimates capitalism and the primacy of profit-making, the "spirit of capitalism."[1]

Stories have long been a key component of the spirit of capitalism. Ascetic Protestants told stories glorifying economic rationalism and the entrepreneur. Benjamin Franklin taught us that "time is money" and that frugality and thrift are virtues demonstrating sound character. The great Captains of Industry told stories about perseverance, vision, and how the "law of competition" would further the human race. These work-as-virtue, profit-as-virtue stories have been remarkably successful. To work for our entire lives seems perfectly natural. That more and more things once

---

1 Luc Boltanski and Eva Chiapello, *The New Spirit of Capitalism*, London: Verso, 2007.

outside the commodity relation are now for sale on the market is something we rarely question.[2]

People have also told stories that challenge capitalism, and, indeed, critiques of capitalism are as old as capitalism itself. The story of the Haymarket Massacre and the anarchists who died fighting for the eight-hour day was told by workers across the globe. In 1886, workers gathered in Haymarket Square in Chicago to protest the killing of several workers by police the previous day. An unknown person threw a bomb at the police as they tried to disperse the crowd, and police responded by firing into the crowd, killing four workers and injuring dozens more. Workers from around the world protested the killings and the sham trial that followed, designating May 1 as International Workers' Day to commemorate the event. In the early years of the twentieth century Joe Hill and other Wobblies travelled the country telling stories and singing songs like "Solidarity Forever" and "The Rebel Girl" about worker solidarity and building "one big union" to unite workers against the bosses. Countless retellings of the bitter campaigns to organize Pullman sleeping car porters and the 1930s autoworker sit-down strikes turned people like A. Philip Randolph and Walter Reuther into working-class heroes.

Stories that challenge the status quo are not just about the economic logic of production, profits, and class struggle. The circuits of power in capitalist society are bolstered by systems

---

2 See Kathi Weeks, *The Problem with Work: Feminism, Marxism, Antiwork Politics, and Postwork Imaginaries*, Durham, N.C.: Duke University Press, 2011.

of oppression and domination that extend beyond class to gender, race, and sexuality. The 1950s and 1960s were alive with stories about the anger of Rosa Parks and Martin Luther King and Malcolm X at Jim Crow and racism. People commiserated with Betty Friedan's frustration with the cult of femininity and listened to stories about Rachel Carson and her quest to curb pesticide use and later about the Oglala Lakota and their standoff with the FBI at Wounded Knee. Throughout the world, stories circulated of emancipation from imperialism, colonialism, and totalitarianism. They gave rise to a larger vision of society, one that looked different from the post–World War II era of Jim Crow, corporate power, exploitation, and domestic domination. By the 1960s and 1970s, the US Congress was implementing watered-down versions of what these movements were demanding, passing unprecedented legislation protecting workers, women, people of color, consumers, and the environment. World leaders bemoaned an "excess of democracy."[3]

This led to a serious crisis of confidence for capital by the late 1970s. Competition had steadily increased in the postwar period, and beginning in the 1960s corporate profit rates stalled and then began to decline at the same time as unemployment was rising and prices were increasing. Many companies stopped investing in new jobs and started investing in finance instead. The grand narrative of progress and

---

3 "The Crisis of Democracy: Report on the Governability of Democracies to the Trilateral Commission," quoted in Noam Chomsky, "The Carter Administration: Myth and Reality," *Australian Quarterly* 50: 1, 1978, 8–36.

modernity led by big companies and the state had become suspect, capitalism no longer seemed to offer the best of all possible worlds, and the state came to be seen as a source of domination and oppression rather than the protector of the common good. As students, workers, women, and people of color continued to demand something different, the crisis deepened and political leaders seemed genuinely uncertain what to do.

New voices emerged to offer guidance. Milton Friedman was one of them, repurposing some very old ideas to argue that the state was the problem. Milton's simple narrative blamed the economic troubles that people found themselves in, and the crisis facing the state, on budget deficits—too much spending that had pushed things out of whack. To get back on course, the state simply needed to stop spending, and to stop listening to the demands for more and better jobs, consumer rights, and protection from the market.

When Ronald Reagan took office in 1980, he used his position to silence dissenting voices and promote a new vision. He told stories about "welfare queens" driving Cadillacs, the "Communist menace" lurking on the horizon, and "getting the government off the backs of the people" through tax cuts and deregulation. He squashed organized labor (breaking the PATCO strike by firing 11,345 air traffic controllers and banning them from future employment in the federal government), weakened environmental protections, and cut funding to agencies tasked with ensuring worker and consumer safety.

Feminist, civil rights, and environmental activists kept fighting, but the powers that be moved with a new, unified force to crush dissent: Organized labor was shaken and class-based movements were discredited. The War on Drugs, followed later by Bill Clinton's Three Strikes law, fuelled an unprecedented trend of mass incarceration that overwhelmingly targeted black and Hispanic men; and the rise of the radical right brought women into direct conflict with each other, focusing feminist battles on holding ground already won rather than embracing more encompassing visions of liberation. The balance of power that had seemed, for a moment in the early 1970s, to favor working people shifted definitively in favor of capital. But the defeats of the 1980s weren't simply a result of capital gathering its forces and stamping out dissent. Proponents of this "counterrevolution" seized on the horrors of Stalinism and repurposed New Left critiques of the repressive apparatus of the state to delegitimize the state, reframing its crucial role in providing a social safety net and regulating corporations as oppressive "big government." Businesses incorporated the demands of workers and students for flexibility and autonomy by replacing the archetypal Company Man with "self-organized," "networked," "creative" individuals with little job security and lots of stress. Companies also found novel ways to undercut unions rather than confront them head on, decentralizing and outsourcing production, offering job security for older workers while eliminating jobs for new workers, and increasing technology to replace workers altogether. In the end, they often simply stopped producing things, opting to earn money through the financial markets instead.

By the 1990s a different kind of capitalism had emerged, one that scholars have described using various terms: post-Fordism, postmodernism, poststructuralism, late capitalism, and even neoliberalism or globalization. The movements of the 1960s and 1970s persisted, but their radical vision had vastly diminished. People began retelling stories about better times, when people were engaged in a vibrant civil society. As sociologist Francesca Polleta argues, many stories treasured by civil rights activists and progressive scholars—such as those told about the Montgomery bus boycott and Freedom Summer—began to serve a commemorative purpose rather than as a blueprint for changing society.[4] Today these stories have even become fodder for the Right: Glenn Beck and Sarah Palin quote Martin Luther King without batting an eyelash.

More important, by the close of the century the stories people told no longer seemed connected to a broader vision of a different society. Life beyond capitalism no longer seemed plausible or even possible. The growing fascination in popular culture and media with apocalyptic narratives and end-of-the-world scenarios reflected a widespread sense that the destruction of society itself seemed more plausible than life after capitalism. The successful absorption and displacement of critique by capital led to confusion, ideological disarray, and an overwhelming sense of fatalism.

Capital's victory in the 1980s brought a surge of profitability and bolstered the power of the elite through massive tax

---

4   Francesca Polletta, *It Was Like a Fever: Storytelling in Protest and Politics*, Chicago: University of Chicago Press, 2006.

cuts, probusiness legislation, and the gutting of the welfare state. But in capitalism halcyon days are always fleeting. As geographer David Harvey says, "Capital doesn't solve its crisis tendencies, it merely moves them around."[5] The booming mid-1990s brought massive income inequality, increased poverty, environmental degradation, skyrocketing levels of consumer debt, persistent gender divides, and widespread anxiety about the future. The 2007/2008 financial meltdown heightened the sense of crisis, and once again questions about the future of capitalism are on the table. According to a 2013 Gallup Poll, 80 percent of Americans are dissatisfied with the way the nation is handling poverty and more than half of the middle class names financial insecurity as their chief concern.[6]

In this moment, a new generation of storytellers has emerged to tell us what's wrong with society and how to fix it. The most powerful of these storytellers aren't poor or working people, they are the super-elite. The loudest critics of capitalism these days are people like Bill Gates, who decries poverty and inequality, and Sheryl Sandberg, who laments persistent gender divides, but they are not calling for an end to capitalism. Instead, they are part of a chorus of new elite voices calling for a different kind of capitalism. The long list of "new" capitalisms being touted or disdained—conscious capitalism, creative capitalism, sustainable capitalism, equitable capitalism, philanthrocapitalism, eco-capitalism,

---

5   David Harvey, "The Enigma of Capital and the Crisis This Time," in Craig Calhoun and Georgi Derluguian, eds., *Business as Usual: The Roots of the Global Financial Meltdown*, New York: New York University Press, 2011.
6   Miles Rapoport and Jennifer Wheary, *Where the Poor and the Middle Class Meet*, New York: Demos, 2013.

inclusive capitalism, crony capitalism—illustrates the widespread feeling that capitalism needs to change.

The New Prophets of Capitalism examines the stories told by four of these new storytellers: Sheryl Sandberg (COO of Facebook), John Mackey (CEO of Whole Foods), Oprah Winfrey (media mogul), and Bill and Melinda Gates (creators of the Gates Foundation).[7] I argue that each of these storytellers acts as a prophet of capitalism. They believe that there are serious problems with capitalism, or with the effects it has on society, and they have a plan or framework the rest of us can use to solve these problems.

What does it mean to be a "prophet" of capitalism? Max Weber defined a prophet as a charismatic individual who, upon receiving a "personal call," embarks on a mission to disseminate a new doctrine—a new vision of how we can enrich our lives and make the world a better place. The prophet's power comes from her personal gifts—her revelations and her charisma. In the pre-industrial era, charisma meant the prophet's ability to demonstrate his powers through using magic or performing miracles. Today's prophets don't perform magic tricks—their charisma comes instead from their capacity to accumulate wealth. Moreover, Weber argues that the key factor distinguishing a prophet from a priest (or a snake-oil salesman) is that the prophet's quest to make people's lives better and solve social problems is unremunerated—she spreads the word free of charge. Oprah

---

7   There are many prophets of capitalism telling stories today. People like Bono and Tom Friedman could easily be added to the list. See the work of Alan Finlayson on "Bonoism."

Winfrey and Melinda Gates don't promote their vision of a better world for personal financial gain. They do it because they want to, because they believe their vision for fixing society's problems is true and effective. Their true believer status, combined with their aura of competence (derived from their "magical" ability to accumulate wealth), gives their stories widespread appeal and makes them prophets.

In certain respects, these new storytellers are indeed similar to prophets past. They draw people to their visions for a better world, and their stories provide both an explanation of, and a solution for, social problems. But these new narratives differ from the popular stories of the 1960s and 1970s, whose visions of life beyond capitalism were discredited along with the social movements from which they grew. Their utopias have been recast as an irrational and hysterical longing. Today's new, elite storytellers present practical solutions to society's problems that can be found within the logic of existing profit-driven structures of production and consumption. They promote market-based solutions to the problems of corporate power, technology, gender divides, environmental degradation, alienation, and inequality. Their visions carry within them a systemic and coherent meaning that seems possible, safe, and achievable within capitalism.

The popular stories told by people like John Mackey and Bill Gates are integral to capitalism, forming the basis of its spirit and providing a vehicle for ideology. Although their perspectives highlight real problems associated with capitalism, like corporate tyranny and environmental degradation, their proposed solutions do not challenge capitalism or its destructive effects. On the contrary, their visions and their solutions bolster capitalism. By offering safe, market-friendly solutions to society's problems the new prophets reinforce the logic and structures of accumulation. Their stories set the terms of debate and the field of possibility, dominating the plane of ideas and swallowing up stories that challenge the status quo. Their stories enable capitalism to evolve and absorb critique, thus preserving itself as a system.

The prophets tell powerful stories and they have the means to make sure they are heard, but this doesn't mean that people always believe their stories or are duped by their message. Ideology is much more subtle. As historian Barbara Fields explains, ideology is the "descriptive vocabulary of day-to-day existence, through which people make rough sense of the social reality that they live and create from day to day."[8] But it is not, philosopher and cultural critic Slavoj Žižek argues, something we can discover and remove from our field of vision, only to reveal the true, nonideological world. Ideology is the world itself, inhabiting and structuring all the spaces in which we live and think.[9]

Oprah, Sheryl Sandberg, and the others are not trying to hide the true structures of power behind our daily interactions. Their stories are a reflection of the capitalist society that already exists, refracted through beliefs and values that already help structure our world. They appeal to common

---

8   Barbara Jeanne Fields, "Slavery, Race and Ideology in the United States of America," *New Left Review* 1:181, 1990, 110.

9   The 2006 film written by and starring Žižek, *A Pervert's Guide to Ideology*, offers a concise explanation of his views on ideology.

narratives and plots and reinforce our current system of values and beliefs. They reference a shared reality that is perfectly aligned with the needs of capital. Challenging these stories would require a fundamental rethinking of our current way of life, a prospect that evokes fears of violence and disorder, and a deeper apprehension that in the process of transforming society we might lose ourselves and the essence of who we are. It would require us to challenge common sense and fight through what sociologist Pierre Bourdieu called our deep-rooted economic fatalism: the "belief that the world cannot be any different from the way it is now."[10]

Part of overcoming economic and political fatalism is critically examining the arguments of these new prophets and understanding their shortcomings. This book is a small attempt at this goal. It draws from the work of talented, dedicated scholars studying development, political economy, ecology, social movements, labor, gender, and education to examine what elite storytellers are telling us and to argue why we should be skeptical of their claims to alleviate poverty, environmental degradation, inequality, and alienation.

I begin by focusing on Facebook COO Sheryl Sandberg's call for women to lean in and seize positions of power and her broader contention that all feminist strategies are compatible with one another. Sandberg is a powerful voice for women and she believes in the feminist project, but her model for liberation won't achieve the goals of feminism. Sandberg's

---

10 Pierre Bourdieu, "A Reasoned Utopia and Economic Fatalism," *New Left Review* 1: 227, 1998, 125–30, quoted in Weeks, *The Problem with Work*, pp. 180–81.

entreaty may work for some women, but on a systemic level it strengthens the forces that oppress and divide women.

Chapter 2 examines eco-capitalism and the growing trend of "sustainable" production and consumption by looking at Whole Foods CEO John Mackey's model of conscious capitalism. Mackey's narrative highlights key problems with the rapid spread of global capitalism and its devastating impact on the environment, but his model fails to challenge the underlying contradictions and imperatives of for-profit production. Human needs can be satiated, but the profit motive cannot—even "sustainable" production in a capitalist system cannot protect the environment from overuse and potentially irreversible damage.

Chapter 3 peels back the layers of media mogul Oprah Winfrey's model of self-help, spiritual capitalism. At a time when the American Dream seems more out of reach than ever, Oprah's message resonates and replicates through all avenues of life. Her helping, healing, self-empowerment message turns up on college campuses, has been adopted by legions of internet entrepreneurs, and is echoed in the vision of organizations like the Freelancers Union. But by emphasizing individual strategies for success, Oprah and other prophets of the empowered self downplay the real structures of power and inequality in our society. They place the burden of success on the individual, in the process disguising societal shortcomings as personal failures and blinding us to collective visions of change that challenge alienation and inequality.

Chapter 4 moves to issues of global poverty and educational reform in the United States through an analysis of the philosophy and practices of the Bill and Melinda Gates Foundation. The confidence and sophistication of the Gates message is seductive. They have powerful connections and deep pockets. They seem not only to know how to fix problems, but also appear to be already doing the fixing. However, instead of alleviating the ills of capitalist markets, the Gates Foundation's policies deepen the reach of capitalist markets to provision of basic human needs such as healthcare and education, and hence reinforce the divide between the rich and the poor.

The final chapter returns to the spirit of capitalism. In this present moment of uncertainty and crisis a new spirit of capitalism is being formulated that incorporates the critiques and ideas of the elite storytellers discussed in this book and around the world. But the new prophets may not have the last word. Social movements are also telling stories and developing projects that radically challenge the capitalist status quo through an emphasis on democracy, de-commodification, and redistribution. These stories and projects foster a new vision of society—a society designed for people instead of profit.

1

Sheryl Sandberg and the Business of Feminism

Fifteen years ago Silicon Valley was inhabited by packs of brogrammers slouching around in hoodies and sandals, hacking code on bean bag chairs, and regurgitating *South Park* jokes. In the intervening years the start-up scene has changed—a bit. Computer technology has been mainstreamed, and women have joined the high-tech gold rush. Tech mammoths like Facebook, IBM, Yahoo!, Hewlett-Packard, and Google all employ women in leading roles.

But despite the power of women like Sheryl Sandberg, Ginni Rometty, Marissa Meyer, Meg Whitman, and Susan Wojcicki, the gender balance in Silicon Valley and the larger corporate world remains highly skewed, and most leadership positions are held by men. At tech companies only 2 to 4 percent of engineers are women; at Fortune 500 firms, 4 percent of CEOs are women. Boardrooms are a bastion of maleness, and many companies, like Twitter, have no women on their board. This disparity extends beyond corporate

America: globally, 90 percent of heads of state are men, and at the 2014 World Economic Forum only 400 of the 2,600 representatives present were women, a 17 percent drop from the previous year. And 2013 marked the first time women held twenty seats in the US Senate.

This is the world into which Sheryl Sandberg, the chief operating officer of Facebook, launched her "sort of manifesto", as she called it, in 2013.[1] *Lean In: Women, Work, and the Will to Lead* addressed the persistent gender imbalance in elite jobs and announced Sandberg's entrance into the century-old struggle for equality in the workplace. From her position of power atop the ping-pong tables and mini-fridges of tech-land, "feminism's new boss" (as Gloria Steinem likes to call her) is exhorting more women to "lean in," scale the "corporate jungle gym," and not stop until they reach the top.

Sandberg's manifesto is a *New York Times* bestseller and has sold over a million and a half copies. Sandberg has been pushing women to be more ambitious for a number of years, through female networking events in Silicon Valley, Women's Leadership Day at Facebook, and monthly dinners for women at her home. In 2010 she extended her message through a TED Talk that went viral, and followed up with an equally popular 2011 commencement speech at Barnard College. *Lean In* revisits and expands the themes in these speeches and argues that women need to stop being afraid and start "disrupting the status quo." "Staying quiet

1   Sheryl Sandberg, *Lean In: Women, Work, and the Will to Lead*, New York: Alfred A. Knopf, 2013.

and fitting in . . . aren't paying off." Instead of waiting for someone to place a tiara on their heads, women need to seize the social and economic gains they want. If they do, Sandberg believes this generation can close the leadership gap and in doing so make the world a better place for all women.[2]

Like many prophets before her, Sandberg makes her case by telling the story of her own path to success. Sandberg worked her way up to the top from middle-class beginnings: her father was an ophthalmologist and her mother was a French teacher turned stay-at-home mom. She graduated from Harvard, twice, and has worked in high-power jobs at the US Treasury, Google, and now Facebook. Industry types consider her a "rock star in business, politics, and popular culture, with unprecedented influence and reach."[3] She is worth more than a billion dollars and was listed at number six on the *Forbes* 2013 Most Powerful Women List, sandwiched between Hillary Clinton and Christine Lagarde of the International Monetary Fund. Sandberg has been so successful at making Facebook profitable that companies want to clone her. Andreessen Horowitz, Facebook board member and cofounder of the Andreessen Horowitz venture capital firm says of Sandberg: "Her name has become a job title. Every company we work with wants a Sheryl."[4]

---

2   Sandberg, *Lean In*, pp. 146–7, 63, 157–8.
3   Miguel Helft, "Sheryl Sandberg: The Real Story," *Forbes*, October 10, 2013.
4   Ibid.

Feminist Ideals and Reality

The runaway success of *Lean In* and, more broadly, the resurgent interest in feminism in wealthy countries, stem from widespread frustration with the advancement of women. Though women in the United States have, roughly speaking, equal rights and access to education, nutrition, and health care as men, the picture for women is disappointing and progress has been slow and halting. Women outperform men in higher education but don't achieve comparable levels of success or wealth. Decisions about balancing home life and work life are as fraught as ever as housing and childcare costs continue to climb. Women are still stereotyped or underrepresented in the popular media—of the 100 highest-grossing 2012 films, only 28.4 percent of speaking characters were women. The backlash against women's reproductive rights continues unabated, with states like Texas passing draconian abortion legislation. After a long, steady decline through the 1990s, rates of violence against women haven't budged since 2005.

For poor women—especially women of color—the situation is far bleaker. Low wage, contingent, and precarious work remains dominated by women. As the income and wealth gap between the rich and poor yawns ever wider, women at the bottom seem to be disappearing from view. The Right doesn't talk about "welfare queens" anymore because state safety net provisions have been all but eliminated and replaced by homeless shelters and food banks. Poor women are more likely to be victims of domestic violence than wealthy women, prevented by poverty and isolation from escaping abusive relationships. A recent report showed that white, female high school dropouts have seen their life expectancy drop by five years over the past two decades.

When Congress passed the Equal Pay Act in 1963, most women, especially those with young children, worked only in the home. In the fifty years since then the situation has reversed. Today 60 percent of women work outside the home. Single and married mothers are even more likely to work, including 57 percent of mothers with children under the age of one. Yet women who work full time still earn only 81 percent of full-time male earnings. This disparity would actually be greater if men's wages (aside from BA degree holders) had not fallen faster than women's in recent years. The wage gap widens when women have children. Women in their early twenties make just over 90 percent of what their male counterparts take home. But between the ages of twenty-five and thirty-four women's relative pay takes a nosedive and continues to decline between thirty-five and forty-four. The divergence illustrates both the unbalanced effect of family care responsibilities and expectations on women and the dramatic effect of pricey childcare and inflexible work schedules on women's earning power.[5]

Surprisingly, the widest pay gaps occur in professional and higher-paying jobs. While this elite job pay gap is in part the result of women "off-ramping" after having children, a

---

5   These data come from an excellent two-part article by Gerald Friedman, "The Wages of Gender," in *Dollars and Sense*, September/October 2013 and November/December 2013.

significant component comes from gatekeeping and professional networks that keep women out of top jobs. When a
female student at Harvard Business School asked William
Boyce, co-founder of Highland Capital Partners, for tips on
entering the venture capital field he laughed and said,
"Don't." Boyce wasn't just channeling Don Draper—he felt
that he was doing the student a solid by letting her in on the
secret that men in finance do not want female peers.[6]

While pay gaps are higher at the top, feminists like bell
hooks argue that sexism and racism pervade all corners of
society. Dominant narratives of power glorify white, heteronormative visions of life. From birth, boys and girls are
treated differently. Assertive girls are called bossy and shamed
for aggressive behavior while boys are expected to take
charge. Girls are given dolls to play with while boys are given
blocks and computer games. Gender stereotypes introduced
in the home, school, and everyday life are perpetuated
throughout women's lives, shaping their identities and life
choices. Men choose higher-paying science and math careers
while women gravitate toward lower-paying, language-
oriented professions.

At the societal level stereotypes intersect with material
conditions to create a gendered, racialized division of labor.
The retail, service, and food sectors—the center of new job
growth—are dominated by women, and the feminization of
"care" work is even more pronounced. Women make up 82
percent of elementary school teachers, 90 percent of nurses,

6   Jodi Kantor, "Harvard Business School Case Study: Gender Equity,"
New York Times, September 7, 2013.

90 percent of housekeepers, 94 percent of child care workers, and 87 percent of personal care workers. In September 2013 President Obama extended the Fair Labor Standards Act to domestic workers (finally), and some states, like California, have passed a domestic worker bill of rights. Despite these significant steps forward, care work is still seen as women's work and undervalued. Disproportionate numbers of caring jobs are low-paying, contingent gigs in which humiliation, harassment, assault, and wage theft are the norm.[7]

Are Women Their Own Worst Enemies?

All feminists recognize the systemic aspects of women's subordination, but some, like Sheryl Sandberg, don't believe that the laundry list of external barriers explains the persistent failure of women to take their rightful place as equal members of society. Sandberg argues that internal barriers are as critical, if not more critical, in explaining women's lives and disappointments.

Betty Friedan exemplified this internal-barriers, get-tough message, and rocked the boat in a big way with her 1963 manifesto *The Feminine Mystique*. Writing near the end of the postwar boom, Friedan discovered that the feminist revolution wasn't over and that women weren't taking advantage of the choices available to them in life. She argued that women in her day often fell victim to "a mistaken choice" between being the "career woman—loveless,

---

7   See www.domesticworkers.org for a series of reports and analyses.

alone" or the "gentle wife and mother—loved and protected by her husband, surrounded by her adoring children."[8] According to Friedan, women were making the wrong choice. Young, educated, middle-class women willingly surrendered to domesticity rather than struggle through the rite-of-passage identity crisis that young men were destined to endure. "It is frightening to grow up finally and be free of passive dependence. Why should a woman bother to be anything more than a wife and mother if all the forces of her culture tell her she doesn't have to, will be better off not to, grow up?"[9]

In her characteristically bold prose Friedan argued that this surrender left a generation of (middle-class, suburban) women with half-formed identities, perpetually stunted and immature, and that domestic escapism often led to depression, bad parenting, adultery, alcoholism, and even suicide. The only way a woman could become a fully formed adult was to get an education and then passionately follow her intellectual interests to a career outside the home.

Sheryl Sandberg is in many respects extending the argument Friedan made, but instead of telling women to get out of the kitchen, Sandberg commands them to get out of the cubicle. She thinks women need to wake up and recognize the invisible, internal forces pushing them down the long, languid road to mediocrity. These internal barriers, while often

8   Betty Friedan, *The Feminine Mystique*, New York: W.W. Norton, 1997 [1963], p. 164.
9   Friedan, *Feminine Mystique*, p. 296.

ignored, are incredibly important, and unlike external barriers, "are under our own control."[10]

Sandberg believes that women talk themselves out of taking power because they feel like frauds and doubt their own capabilities, and because they face resistance from a culture that penalizes "aggressive and hard-charging" women who "violate unwritten rules about acceptable social conduct."[11] Women worry so much about work/life balance and whether "having it all" (family and career) is really possible that they often give up before they have to, putting their foot on the brakes when they should be putting their foot on the gas. Women still face a "mistaken choice":

> women are surrounded by headlines and stories warning them that they cannot be committed to both their families and careers. They are told over and over again that they have to choose, because if they try to do too much, they'll be harried and unhappy. Framing the issue as "work-life balance"—as if the two were diametrically opposed—practically ensures work will lose out. Who would ever choose work over life?[12]

Women's decisions to give up on their ambitions as adults are often the result of learned dispositions and habits acquired during childhood. But despite this socialization and its long-term effects, Sandberg doesn't really believe in glass ceilings

---

10 Sandberg, *Lean In*, p. 9.
11 Ibid., p. 17.
12 Ibid., p. 23.

or see the need for affirmative action. She thinks the main force holding women back—at least educated women—is their own hang-ups and fears. Women don't need favors, they just need to believe in themselves. "Fear is at the root of so many of the barriers that women face . . . Without fear, women can pursue professional success and personal fulfillment."[13] Deborah Gruenfeld calls Sandberg a post-feminist—a woman who believes that "when you blame someone else for keeping you back, you are accepting your powerlessness."[14]

So how should women take power and the corner office? Women must face their fears, be aggressive, sit at the table, raise their hands, and not put them down until they're called upon. That's what men do, after all. Women must be cognizant of biases against women and adjust their strategies—"think personally, act communally"—and give legitimate explanations for their negotiation demands. They must choose the right partner—someone willing to share dreams and dishes. The bad boys are fun, but for God's sake, don't marry them. Most important, women must zero in on growth and seize opportunities—both in the company they choose to work for and in their personal lives. Sandberg says that she decided to join Google in 2001 over other firms that were more of a sure thing because Eric Schmidt likened it to a rocket ship. "Over the years [she has] repeated Eric's advice to countless people, encouraging them to reduce

---

13   Sandberg, *Lean In*, pp. 24–5.
14   Ken Auletta, "A Woman's Place: Can Sheryl Sandberg Upend Silicon Valley's Male-Dominated Culture?" *New Yorker*, July 11, 2011.

their career spreadsheets to one column: potential for growth."[15]

Women of the World Unite . . . and Take Power!

Sandberg's manifesto has struck a chord with women, at least in the United States. Some of the popularity of *Lean In* can be chalked up to Sandberg's access to a massive media machine, but its acclaim reflects widespread concern among women, and society more broadly, about questions of feminism and women's rights.

At its peak, the 1970s women's movement was a dynamic social force that "wove together . . . three analytically distinct dimensions of gender injustice: economic, cultural, and political."[16] Since then, mainstream interest in feminism has ebbed and flowed, and the broad feminist platform has split, branching off in noncontiguous directions. In the 1980s most core feminist theorizing migrated to academia and turned to questions of culture and identity, while the broader movement battled attacks on reproductive rights. The 1990s saw a renewed interest in "girl power" and emergent strands of radical feminism, through zine and Riot Grrl culture, and the 2000s saw a rapid proliferation of "ladybloggers."

These days, despite the reluctance of many women to identify as feminists, the woman question is once again in the air. A spate of new books and articles, by both young and old

---

15 Sandberg, *Lean In*, p. 58.
16 Nancy Fraser, "Feminism, Capitalism, and the Cunning of History," *New Left Review* 2: 56, 2009, 98.

feminists are receiving attention from all corners. Splashy projects like Femen and SlutWalk are raising eyebrows and making headlines, and modern-day consciousness-raising projects like Laura Bates's Everyday Sexism blog and the Who Needs Feminism tumblr page have proven remarkably popular. The topic of women's rights in the Global South has also seen increasing passion and interest over the past two decades, though the plight of women in poor countries often plays second fiddle to concerns about violence, pornography, and reproductive rights that dominate Western feminist agendas and budgets.

Lean In earned widespread praise in the mainstream presses, but not everyone was keen on Sandberg's stop-holding-yourself-back narrative. In an article for *Dissent*, Sarah Jaffe argued that feminists should stop obsessing over "the travails of some of the world's most privileged women" because in real life "most women are up against a wall." As the recovery from the Great Recession drags on, more women are finding themselves out of work or forced to get by on a Walmart salary. Jaffe notes that "this is where most women spend their time, not atop the Googleplex. This is where feminists should be spending their time, too."[17]

Sandberg assures her readers that she is "acutely aware" of the external obstacles to gender equality and knows that most women are struggling to get by, not get the corner office.

---

17   Sarah Jaffe, "Trickle-Down Feminism," *Dissent*, Winter 2013. bell hooks also criticized Sandberg for privileging a white, heteronormative vision of relationships and family.

However, she claims that the argument is misguided, since
the divide between feminists is "the ultimate chicken-and-
egg situation":

> The chicken: Women will tear down the external barriers
> once we achieve leadership roles. We will march into our
> bosses' offices and demand what we need . . . Or better
> yet, we'll become bosses and make sure all women have
> what they need. The egg: we need to eliminate the exter-
> nal barriers to get women into those roles in the first
> place.[18]

In other words, it's not the chicken *or* the egg, it's the chicken
and the egg: "Both sides are right." By arguing, we just hold
each other back. Some feminists can pursue the institutional-
change-first route, while others (like herself) can pursue the
take-power-first route. "Rather than engage in philosophical
arguments over which comes first, let's agree to wage battles
on both fronts" and meet together on the other side. Together
all the efforts of women will add up to a better world for
women.[19]

The important thing for Sandberg is that women take
power by any means necessary. She says she was blind to this
problem when she was younger because she thought the
feminists had won and that it was "just a matter of time until
her generation took its share of leadership roles."[20] But now

---

18   Sandberg, *Lean In*, pp. 8–9.
19   Sandberg, *Lean In*, pp. 8–9.
20   Ibid., p. 7.

that she's reached the top, she often finds herself the only woman in the room.

Sandberg argues that women face many of the problems they do because men hold positions of power and women's voices are not heard. If women can gain an equal share of leadership roles they can speak for all women. Sandberg illustrates her point through a story from her time at Google. One day when she was very, very pregnant, Sandberg found herself in agony, huffing and puffing across the vast Google parking lot. In that moment it dawned on her that, dammit, Google needed pregnant woman parking. She marched into her boss's office and demanded it. "Having one pregnant woman at the top—even one who looked like a whale—made the difference." Sandberg is no longer pregnant, or working at Google, but the pregnancy parking has remained. Sandberg tells her parking space story because the experience illuminated what women need. "Conditions for all women will improve when there are more women in leadership roles giving strong and powerful voice to their needs and concerns." Every time someone like Sandberg marches into the boss's office with a demand, or, ideally, becomes the boss, the world will get a little better for women. "The shift to a more equal world will happen person by person. We move closer to the larger goal of true equality with each woman who leans in."[21]

Sandberg's emphasis on taking power is shared widely among advocates for gender equality. A recent UK initiative

---

21   Ibid., pp. 4, 7, 11.

called the Fabian Women's Network is pushing the same line. The network's mission is to facilitate the participation of women in politics and public life through its mentoring program and networking events. As one participant of the program said, "The privately educated, white middle-class males have had bridges to power built for hundreds of years. It's time for women and ethnic minorities to build their own bridges."[22]

In an influential 2012 article in the *Atlantic* Anne-Marie Slaughter argues that she once thought women could "have it all," but that after working a job with fixed hours (as director of policy planning at the State Department) she realized she was dead wrong. Not only was Slaughter mistaken, she laments how for many years her public persona and speeches were deaf to the challenges facing young women today: "I'd been part, albeit unwittingly, of making millions of women feel that *they* are to blame if they cannot manage to rise up the ladder as fast as men and also have a family and an active home life (and be thin and beautiful to boot)." Slaughter argues that the way the economy and society are structured today makes it all but impossible for women to meet both their family and career needs satisfactorily. In most jobs women have no control over their schedules. When problems arise at home (as they often do with children) something has to give and for many women that something is their career ambitions.[23] However, while Slaughter may disagree with

---

22   Yvonne Roberts, "Mentoring Scheme Gives Women Keys to Gates of Power, *Guardian*, September 18, 2013.
23   Anne-Marie Slaughter, "Why Women Still Can't Have It All," *Atlantic*, June 13, 2012.

Sandberg about women having it all today, she believes that *someday* women could have it all. But that someday will require women to "close the leadership gap; to elect a woman president and 50 women senators; to ensure that women are equally represented in the ranks of corporate executives and judicial leaders. Only when women wield power in sufficient numbers will we create a society that genuinely works for all women."[24]

At a recent speech for the Clinton Global Initiative, Hillary Clinton argued that women are the world's most "underused resource." Warming up for a potential 2016 presidential bid, Clinton declared that the need for more female participation in public life and politics is a "no-brainer": "When women participate in the economy, everyone benefits. When women participate in peacemaking and peacekeeping, we are all safer and more secure. And when women participate in politics, the effects ripple out across society."[25]

The taking power strategy has bridged many divides in feminism, and there's no doubt that women, especially women of color, need to move into positions of power. Take power arguments are also appealing for activists because they offer a tangible, manageable goal. Over the past four decades women have slowly pushed into spheres and roles that once seemed impossible. With a bit more hard work it seems possible to close the leadership gap. Sandberg certainly believes

24   Ibid.
25   Jennifer Skalka Tulumello, "Hillary Clinton Makes a Splash in Chicago, But Not an Overtly Political One," *Christian Science Monitor*, June 13, 2013.

so: "The hard work of generations before us means that equality is within our reach . . . If we push hard now, this next wave can be the last wave. In the future, there will be no female leaders. There will just be leaders."[26]

But the argument rests on the problematic assumption that women are inherently, or because of cultural training, more decent than men, and that ladies look out for each other. Those who lived through the reign of Margaret Thatcher can attest to the flaws in this argument.

Marissa Mayer, Sandberg's former comrade at Google, is a shining example of a woman who leaned in to power and influence. Mayer became the first pregnant CEO ever when she took the helm at Yahoo! in the summer of 2012. But instead of using her powerful position to help women, Mayer used it to cut 30 percent of Yahoo's workforce and eliminate flextime, an arrangement that allowed hundreds of Yahoo workers to work from home one or two days a week so they could care for children, elderly parents, etc. Running against the grain of recent productivity research, Mayer argued that face-time trumps flextime: "Speed and quality are often sacrificed when we work from home ... Some of the best decisions and insights come from hallway and cafeteria discussions, meeting new people, and impromptu team meetings."[27] Flextime was a long-standing policy at Yahoo. Many people (women in particular) chose the company over other tech companies

---

26 Sandberg, *Lean In*, pp. 171–2.
27 Kara Swisher, "'Physically Together': Here's the Internal Yahoo No-Work-from-Home Memo for Remote Workers and Maybe More," *All Things D*, February 22, 2–13.

because it offered this option, but because Mayer was the boss she could eliminate the policy with a stroke of her keyboard.

This anecdote is not meant to make Mayer look bad. It simply highlights a problem with the core idea of Sandberg, and many other prominent feminists, that putting women in power is the key to improving the lives of all women. The person in power is the boss. She gets to do pretty much whatever she wants. If she wants to put in pregnancy parking, great. If she wants to get rid of flextime she can do that, too. As Pulitzer Prize–winning journalist Susan Faludi wrote, "You can't change the world for women by simply inserting female faces at the top of an unchanged system of social and economic power." Or, as activist and author Charlotte Bunch once quipped, "You can't just add women and stir."[28]

Our Bodies, Ourselves . . . for Capital

The problems with Sandberg's story run deeper than her belief in sisterly solidarity. Of central concern is the dominant message of *Lean In*—that women's road to self-actualization and equality lies in the "perpetual acceleration of one's own labor," in the constant quest to grow and the bestowal of the fruits of that growth on their employers. In this formulation the growth of the company and the growth of the worker become inseparable.[29]

---

28 Susan Faludi, "Sandberg Left Single Mothers Behind," *CNN Opinion*, March 13, 2013.

29 Kate Losse, "Feminism's Tipping Point: Who Wins from Leaning In?" *Dissent*, March 26, 2013.

Both Sandberg and Mayer had (relatively) generous paid maternity leave, but Mayer chose not to use hers, and Sandberg used only part of hers. Both women felt intense pressure to get back to work to display their commitment to their companies and the projects they were working on. Sandberg says that women should try to be home for dinner with their children every night, but she fully accepts the "new normal" of working tirelessly before work, during work, and after work. "Facebook is available around the world 24/7, and for the most part, so [is she]. The days when [Sandberg] even thinks of unplugging for a weekend or vacation are long gone."[30]

Sandberg is in good company: feminism has attached itself to the question of work for over a century. Betty Friedan, and many others, put wage work on a pedestal as the ultimate means for social expression and status attainment. But this one-to-one mapping of feminism onto wage work is potentially problematic for emancipatory strategies. Political scientist Kathi Weeks argues that while the struggle for "more and better work" is crucial, it is also important to consider how the "valorization of work" dominates "feminist analytical frames and political agendas."[31] For Weeks, the work ethic— the tight normative linkage between wage work and happiness, success, status, and self-worth—produces a human whose hopes, desires, beliefs, and acts all orbit around the centrality of work.[32] The effect of Sandberg's narrative of

---

30 Sandberg, *Lean In*, pp. 133–4.
31 Weeks, *The Problem with Work*, p. 152.
32 Ibid., p. 54.

self-improvement is to channel women's whole selves—the sum of their energies and desires—toward working harder and longer. It makes women "believe their labor serves the self and not the marketplace."[33]

The point at issue is not that *Lean In* touts hard work, but rather that it presents scaling the corporate jungle gym as the solution to the problem of gender inequality: the *Lean In* story isn't just a personal instruction sheet for how to win friends and influence people, it is a manifesto, an action plan, that argues all feminist strategies are compatible with one another. But they are not, and feminist ideals cannot be achieved if they are pursued Sandberg-style. Women who channel their energies toward reaching the top of corporate America undermine the struggles of women trying to realize institutional change by organizing unions and implementing laws that protect women (and men) in the workplace.

An anecdote shared by Sandberg illustrates this point: In 2010 Mark Zuckerberg pledged $100 million to improve the performance metrics of the Newark Public Schools. The money would be distributed through a new foundation called Startup: Education. Sandberg recommended Jen Holleran, a woman she knew "with deep knowledge and experience in school reform" to run the foundation. The only problem was that Jen was raising fourteen-month-old twins at the time, working part time, and not getting much help from her husband. Jen hesitated to accept the offer, fearful of "upsetting the current order" at home. But with Sandberg's urging,

---

33   Maya Tokumitsu, "In the Name of Love," *Jacobin* 13, 2013.

she ultimately decided to "take the job because of the impact it would have." Her husband stepped up to the plate and took on more household responsibilities and childcare, and now "Jen loves her job and is glad that she and her husband have a more equal marriage."[34]

Things worked out great for Jen Holleran, but the position she leaned into undermines the position of hundreds of other women—Newark school teachers. A core goal of Startup: Education was to institute a merit pay program for Newark's teachers. The program, which Sandberg played a central role in designing, rewarded "highly effective" teachers who produced high standardized test scores with bonuses while simultaneously putting teachers whose students performed poorly on track for disciplinary action or dismissal.[35]

Hundreds of teachers who have been deemed "unsatisfactory" are being kept on payroll as substitute teachers and rotated between Newark's seventy schools while city officials and Newark school reformers use Startup and other funds to develop a buyout program similar to programs used in New York and Houston. The long-term goal is to reduce the number of tenured teachers, keep the remaining ones on their toes with merit pay and weakened tenure rights, and bring in new short-term teachers through programs like Teach For America.

Jen Holleran achieved success at work and fulfillment at home, but her personal gain came at the expense of other

---

34   Sandberg, *Lean In*, p. 117.
35   Jenny Brown, "Lean In or Stand Up," *Labor Notes*, November 4, 2013.

women trying to defend their own gains and improve their schools in a complex, difficult environment. Her story highlights how the pursuit of individual success within the existing structures of social and economic power can be great for one woman, but on a broader scale undermine the struggles of other women and bolster the gendered and racialized division of labor in our society.

Feminism as Ideology: The Need for a Collective Vision

The enthusiasm of Fortune 500 companies like Walmart (a company sued for discrimination against women) for the *Lean In* message demonstrates how neatly Sandberg's story dovetails with companies' desire to have bright, hard-working, ambitious employees. Women's success makes the existing agenda of corporate power appear both just and justified. By providing a pathway for women to advance and mouthing their support for vague notions of gender equality, companies, and the broader capitalist economy, appear meritocratic and even benevolent—a place where anyone (man or woman) who works hard enough will succeed.

As we have seen over the past three decades of neoliberalism, globalization, and financialization, the tendency within capitalism is to polarize not unite, to create divisions not equality. Capitalism has inherent contradictions that pit workers against the companies that employ them and against each other. Workers' wages come directly from the profits of companies. When competition between firms increases (as it always does) companies look to their wage bill for savings by paying their workers less, slashing their benefits, and making them work harder and longer.

Meanwhile, capital feeds on existing norms of sexism and racism, compounding the exploitative nature of wage work. When women's ambitions and desires are silenced or under-valued, they are easier to take advantage of. Sexism and racism are part of the company toolkit, enabling firms to pay women less—particularly women of color—discriminate against them, steal their wages, and treat them badly. But even if we root out sexism and racism, the inherent contra-dictions of capitalism will persist. Putting women in charge will not change the power of the profit motive and the compulsion of companies to give workers as little as economic, social, and cultural norms will allow.

The goal of feminism is justice and equality for all women, not simply equal opportunity for women or equal participa-tion by women. By aligning the goals of feminism with the goals of capitalism, Sandberg's model of emancipation func-tions as ideology, accepting and undergirding the dominant structures of power in society. Her critique of gender inequal-ity in elite jobs, while accurate and thoughtful, glorifies the capitalist work ethic by pushing women to seek self-actualization through self-exploitation. Women who follow her action plan may achieve more success in their careers, and perhaps even reach the heights that Sandberg herself has gained. But her plan will help only a small number of women—the women who can find a place within the limited number of power positions in the corporate hierarchy. Everyone else—the domestic workers, retail staff, caregivers—will remain excluded, their efforts undermined by the strengthening of capital and the women who burnish its meritocratic facade.

At the same time, alternative visions will be silenced. Sandberg's power as a billionaire prophet with access to an enormous media empire allows her voice and vision to dominate the limited space available in public discussions about women, drowning out radical stories that challenge the status quo and call attention to how class, race, and gender intersect to create deep disparities in wealth and well-being in our society.

Sandberg is right that women hold themselves back as a result of patriarchal norms that push them to be caring and nice. Women do need to stop worrying about being perfect mothers/wives/daughters. Women do need to take the lead and enter positions of power. This part of her story needs to be shared and internalized. But Sandberg's version of leaning in reinforces the fundamentally exploitative social relations that characterize our society and strengthen a system that permanently divides women at the top from women at the bottom.

If we truly want to realize the goals of our mothers and sisters struggling through the ages and make the world a better place for women, we need to lean in to campaigns and projects that challenge existing structures of power. If we're going to improve women's lives we need to help them organize their workplaces. While it might work for some women (like Sandberg) to focus on individual strategies to get ahead in their jobs, the only way most women are going to get sick days, family leave, health insurance, or a raise is through a collective bargaining agreement organized with other workers, not "trickle-down feminism."[36] Women must lean in to collective projects that unite women in spirit and purpose, projects that channel individual female voices into a deafening roar for true feminism, projects that give women the power to change the world, to make it a better place for all people.

---

36   Marilyn Sneiderman, quoted in Jaffe, *Dissent*, 2013.

2

Capital's Id: Whole Foods, Conscious Capitalism and Sustainability

John Mackey spent his formative years trying to divine the purpose of his life. After much soul-searching and lots of reading, he made an important decision: come hell or high water "he would follow his heart wherever it led him." Since 1980 his heart has led him to create and run Whole Foods Market—"a store that sells healthy food to people and provides good jobs." More recently, Mackey has embarked on a grander mission: "to liberate the extraordinary power of business and capitalism to create a world in which all people live lives full of prosperity, love, and creativity—a world of compassion, freedom, and prosperity."[1]

---

1   John Mackey and Raj Sisodia, *Liberating the Heroic Spirit of Business: Conscious Capitalism*, Boston, MA.: Harvard Business Review Press, 2013. This book is the primary reference for "conscious capitalism" in this chapter. It is co-written by Mackey and Sisodia, alternating between a first-person Mackey voice and a joint Mackey/Sisodia voice. My interest lies in the story Mackey tells about Whole Foods, and because the book is primarily about Whole Foods and builds on previous discussions of conscious capitalism developed by Mackey, I refer only to Mackey in this chapter. The reader should note, however, that general views about conscious capitalism are shared and developed by Sisodia.

Mackey is not your typical CEO. He hasn't taken a paycheck for more than six years. He has also donated all his recent stock options to Whole Planet, a Whole Foods nonprofit that provides start-up microloans to poor people (primarily women) in more than fifty developing countries. Mackey drives his early model Prius to work every day on a mission: He wants the planet to eat better, and he wants to teach other entrepreneurs the secrets of "conscious capitalism." He believes that if businesspeople, and society more broadly, realize the incredible power of "conscious" businesses to create value and heal the planet, we can reverse the missteps of the past few decades.

A growing consensus is emerging that the spread of global capitalism, while profitable for some people and institutions, is seriously harming poor people and the planet itself. Rising inequality and environmental degradation are bringing into question capitalism's ability to produce secure livelihoods without destroying the planet in the process. Mackey thinks the behavior of capitalists hasn't helped matters. He believes businesses that focus on short-term profits rather than long-term growth do more harm than good and give capitalism a bad name. Instead, companies need to break free from this model and reveal the "beautiful," "heroic" spirit of free-market capitalism. Companies that have a mission and passionately follow it by encouraging creativity and honoring all stakeholders (customers, workers, suppliers, investors, communities, and the environment) are what society needs to solve the problems of environmental degradation and social inequality and restore the image of capitalism.

This mission has transformed Whole Foods into something bigger than pyramids of shiny pink ladies and regiments of straight-shooting asparagus. The company donates 5 to 10 percent of its profits every year to nonprofits like the Whole Kids program, an initiative designed to improve nutrition and wellness for schoolchildren. Whole Kids puts salad bars in schools, provides nutrition information to school staff, and funds school garden projects; elementary schools in numerous states, including California, Alabama, Ohio, and Oregon, have planted school gardens through the program. Its Whole Cities program is tackling the challenge of urban "food deserts" by providing grants and educational resources to community groups in cities like New Orleans and Jackson, Mississippi. Whole Foods is also a leader in the supermarket field on the ethical treatment of animals: It is a member of the Global Animal Partnership and claims that it uses a rigorous, five-step rating system to promote ethical animal agricultural practices.[2]

Whole Foods' "core values" extend beyond philanthropic gestures and selling ethically produced, organic food. The company says that it seeks to honor all stakeholders from suppliers to communities, and from workers to the environment. It provides logistical support and low-interest loans to "independent, local farms" and "food artisans," and gives small businesses a platform for increasing sales through its stores. In a retail world dominated by low-road employers like Walmart and McDonalds, Whole Foods bucks the trend

---

2 See www.wholefoodsmarket.com/.

by offering higher wages, a decent health care plan, and a voice to workers to improve their workplace. Leadership structures are decentralized, giving local stores and individual "team members" more autonomy in organizing work patterns, and all workers have access to the company's employment statistics. They can see how much every person in the company, including Mackey himself, makes. And, while the salaries of US corporate executives have skyrocketed over the past two decades, the company has restrained executive pay to nineteen times the average pay of all team members ($18 an hour for full-time, permanent employees). By comparison, in 2011 Apple's Tim Cook took home $378 million in salary, stock, and other benefits, which was 6,258 times the pay of an average Apple employee.

How can Whole Foods do all these things and remain profitable in the cutthroat food industry, where most food retailers make profits of pennies on the dollar? Although Whole Foods saw a temporary dip in profits following the 2008 financial crisis, Mackey attributes the long-term prosperity of the company to its conscious growth model. He believes that the model has led to a different kind of enterprise, one able to withstand the storms of competition through creativity and innovation. By honoring all its stakeholders, Whole Foods creates an "operating system" that is "in harmony with the fundamentals of human nature" and the planet.[3]

Mackey is not alone. His 2013 book, *Conscious Capitalism: Liberating the Heroic Spirit of Business* (co-authored with Raj

---

3   Mackey and Sisodia, *Conscious Capitalism*, p. 236.

Sisodia), is a *New York Times* and *Wall Street Journal* bestseller. *Forbes* calls it an inspiration for CEOs, and Oprah featured the book on her Super Soul Sunday show. Other companies and entrepreneurs have joined the "conscious capitalism" movement.[4] They argue that the old business paradigms based on zero-sum thinking are not working. If society is to avoid the devastating environmental and social effects of the current trajectory it needs to take a different path. Mackey believes that this is starting to happen, and though this nascent philosophy of capitalism is in its early stages, the direction is clear: "If your company doesn't care, it will not be in business for long."[5]

The Anthropocene Era

For the past thirty years companies have been told that their only social responsibility is to make a profit. In this ideological context, recent moves by mega-corporations like Kraft, Walmart, McDonalds, Hewlett-Packard, Nordstrom, Nestlé, IKEA, Southwest Airlines, Zappos, and many more to scrutinize their supply chains and speed their adoption of sustainable practices is surprising and indicates growing concerns about the current global model of extraction, production, distribution, and consumption.

In 1972 researchers at MIT published their eye-opening study *The Limits to Growth*. The project used computer

---

4   For example, see Michael Strong, *Be the Solution: How Entrepreneurs and Conscious Capitalists Can Solve All the World's Problem's*, New York: Wiley, 2009.

5   Mackey and Sisodia, *Conscious Capitalism*, pp. 264–5, 230.

simulations to demonstrate the potentially devastating impact of exponential capitalist growth in a closed system with finite resources. Examining growth trends in human population, industrialization, pollution, and resource depletion, the report's authors suggested possible scenarios of "overshoot and collapse" in the global system by the middle of the twenty-first century. In the decades since, a shared global consciousness has emerged that humans are destroying the planet. Some scientists have even started referring to the time since the rise of industrial capitalism as the Anthropocene era, arguing that humans are altering the planet in ways similar to major geological events in the past.

Apocalyptic predictions about the effects of global warming have become a news staple as groups like the Natural Resources Defense Council broadcast a steady stream of warnings about a future plagued by droughts, typhoons, fires, and floods. Freshwater bodies like the Ogallala Aquifer (beneath the Great Plains in the United States) and the Aral Sea (between Kazakhstan and Uzbekistan) are being rapidly depleted, and scientists estimate that 40 percent of the ocean's waters are "heavily affected" by human activities. Overuse of water is matched by dramatic transformations in the planet's cultivable land area. According to the UN Food and Agricultural Organization, 30 percent of the Earth's land is now devoted to supporting livestock for consumption. Extinction rates for wild animals are hundreds and even thousands of times higher than "background rates" in the fossil record, with large predators most threatened. Scientists estimate that the wild population of vertebrates has declined 30 percent since 1970, mainly due to habitat loss.[6]

Westerners have a particularly large ecological footprint. US consumers ranked last in a seventeen-country survey of sustainable behavior conducted by National Geographic. Despite having only 5 percent of the global population, the United States accounts for 25 percent of the world's coal consumption, 26 percent of oil, and 27 percent of natural gas. Our homes and cars are bigger, and per capita we consume more than anyone else on the planet. Thanks to household water use (flushing toilets, washing clothes) and "embodied" water in food production (like coffee and meat), a child born in the United States uses 30 to 50 times more water than a child born in a developing country and creates 13 times more ecological damage in the course of her lifetime. One American adult drains more resources than 35 Indians and buys 53 times more goods and services than someone in China.[7]

Outsized consumption patterns are only a part of the problem. Many environmental groups blame dominant conceptions of economic growth that focus on gross domestic product (GDP) as a measure of prosperity without considering the effects of constantly expanding production and consumption on the environment. Groups like Greenpeace and Rainforest Action Network argue that the

6 *People and the Planet Report*, Report 01/12, London: Royal Society Science Policy Centre, 2012.
7 "Use It and Lose It: The Outsize Effect of US Consumption on the Environment," *Scientific American*, September 14, 2012.

unfettered access of transnational corporations to the riches of the planet—underwritten by institutions like the World Trade Organization—is destroying the world's air, water, and land.

"Maligned" and "Misunderstood": It's Not Capitalism's Fault!

Mackey agrees that the destructive actions of big corporations obsessed with the bottom line have damaged the environment, but he vehemently denies that the problem is capitalism. Mackey argues that true capitalism, or free-enterprise capitalism (free markets + free people), is a unique, inherently virtuous system that, properly harnessed, can heal the planet.

Critics of capitalism say it is an exploitative, zero-sum system in which the riches of some depend on the impoverishment of others. Mackey disagrees. He argues that capitalism is actually based on freedom, not coercion or exploitation. It is a system in which "people trade voluntarily for mutual gain." Workers, customers, investors, and suppliers all have the freedom to trade with whomever they wish. If people don't like what a company sells, they can shop elsewhere. If workers don't like the way a company treats its employees, they can find a different job. But when investors, labor, management, and suppliers choose to cooperate, they can create unprecedented value. In a free market, this joint value is "divided fairly among the creators of the value through competitive market processes based approximately on the overall contribution each stakeholder makes. In other words, business is not a zero-sum game with a winner and a loser. It is a win, win, win, win game."[8]

Sure, companies have been misbehaving recently, but before we throw the baby out with the bathwater, Mackey implores us to remember that most of the wonderful things we have in the world, like cars, computers, antibiotics, and the internet, are a product of free markets, not "government edict." The "wondrous technologies that have shrunk time and distance" and freed us from "mindless drudgery" have become possible only because of free market capitalism— "unquestionably the greatest system for innovation and social cooperation that has ever existed."[9]

Instead of blaming capitalism for inequality and environmental degradation, Mackey suggests that we should look at the actions of governments. Departing from the dominant idea that states have retreated from the market over the past three decades, Mackey argues states have become more interventionist than ever, and that in the process they have "fostered a mutant form of capitalism called crony capitalism" that is to blame for many of the problems societies face today. Mackey does not see crony capitalism as "real" capitalism. Instead it is a product of big government in which politicians trying to preserve their cushy jobs develop symbiotic, parasitic relationships with businesspeople too lazy or unimaginative to compete successfully in the marketplace.[10]

---

8   Mackey and Sisodia, *Conscious Capitalism*, p. 3.
9   Ibid., pp. 14, 27.
10   Ibid., pp. 16, 21; Mackey is not alone in his emphasis on crony capitalism. See also www.againstcronycapitalism.org/.

In Mackey's story, crony capitalism has been exacerbated by the rising power of the financial sector and shareholder-value ideology—the idea that firms are nothing more than a stream of assets designed to maximize profits for shareholders. Mackey argues that this obsession with greed and profits has "robbed most businesses of their ability to engage and connect with people" and has created "long-term systemic problems" that destroy profitability and that can be deeply damaging to people and to the planet. "Too many businesses fail to recognize the significant impacts they have on the environment, on other creatures that inhabit the planet (such as wildlife and livestock animals), and on the physical health and psyches of team members and customers."[11]

Instead of trying to get a handout from the government or make a quick buck on the stock market, Mackey says that companies need to roll up their sleeves and rethink how to run a business. The first thing they need to do is to realize that a business is a "social system," not a hierarchy.[12] Everyone matters. A company can squeeze its workers or screw over its suppliers to get a bump in quarterly sales and a boost in share price. With luck, it might rake in profits for quite a while by taking these shortcuts, but in the long run it will lose and harm everyone and everything around it.

---

11   Ibid., pp. 16, 18.
12   Charles. Fishman, "Whole Foods Is All Teams," *Fast Company*, April/May1996.

The Consumer-Citizen

Mackey's vision of a helping, healing company has been embraced by Whole Foods consumers and has generated an extremely devoted customer base. In a recent survey, US and Canadian consumers ranked Whole Foods first among stores providing healthy, high-quality food.[13] One of Mackey's favorite memories is the support and encouragement he received from customers and neighbors after a massive flood all but destroyed the first Whole Foods store in Austin, Texas, in 1981. The flood left the store under eight feet of dirty water, ruining all the inventory and equipment inside and, it seemed at the time, Mackey's dreams. But after the water receded, dozens of loyal customers showed up, unbeckoned, with mops and buckets ready to help get the store up and running again because they loved it so much. The company is no less popular today. It relies heavily on word-of-mouth advertising, and even in a food mecca like New York City, customers lined up around the block to enter Whole Foods' 59,000-square-foot mega-store in Columbus Circle when it opened in 2003.

The devotion and loyalty displayed by Whole Foods customers, and, more broadly, the growing demand for organic, sustainable food, are indicative of the changing complexion of the global environmental movement. Until the early 1990s the environmental movement was combative and largely targeted producers. Global and grassroots environmental groups focused their energies on getting states,

13   'Trader Joe's Top Survey of Best Grocery Chains, Walmart Lands at Bottom of List," *Huffington Post*, July 23, 2013.

networks of states, and intergovernmental bodies like the United Nations to implement restrictions to stop companies from dumping toxic waste in streams and rivers, clear-cutting forests, and belching exhaust into the atmosphere.

Over the past decade and a half, this state-centered focus has shifted to a consumer-centered focus as fears stoked by globalization have changed the frame of environmentalism. In the age of global supply chains, free trade agreements, and capital flight, states have increasingly come to be seen as incapable of protecting their citizens from big global problems like ozone depletion, climate change, and biodiversity loss, and even more tractable problems, like controlling hazardous waste flows or regulating toxic substances in consumer goods.[14]

But while processes of globalization have delegitimized states and made citizens feel disconnected from the protective embrace of their respective governments, they have also helped to forge new, global identities based on feelings of "world-citizenship."[15] Westerners in particular have become uneasily aware of their power as consumers in shaping and driving global value chains. Whereas in the past consumers were considered "small polluters" relative to the big industrial polluters, in recent years this view has changed. Current global frameworks of environmental power place consumers on an equal plane with states, corporations, and civil-society actors.

---

14   Gert Spaargaren and Arthur P.J. Mol, "Greening Global Consumption: Redefining Politics and Authority," *Global Environmental Change* 18, 2008, 350–9.
15   John Boli and George Thomas, "World Culture in the World Polity: A Century of International Non-Governmental Organization," *American Sociological Review* 62: 2, April 1997, 171–90.

This newfound perception conflates consumption with politics and citizenship and has led to the widespread adoption of "ecological consumerism" and "lifestyle politics" as expressions of environmental awareness and concern. Sociologist Josée Johnston attributes the popularity of consumption politics, in part, to the fact that it's really easy. "Exercising consumer choice appears as both a viable and convenient strategy—particularly when compared to the onerous demands of social movement organizing or trade unionism."

Lifestyle politics also provides an extremely wide scope for expressing more general feelings of angst and unhappiness with "late" capitalism. People who are stressed about personal debt, aghast at unfair trade policies, or newly interested in free food movements and global social justice are told they can make a difference by buying better things like organic food and sustainably produced furniture. "By harnessing the power of consumer choice, ethical consumption appears to shape the market in a way that preserves the environment, addresses poverty, and promotes democracy." In the ethical consumption framework the consumer-citizen becomes a powerful agent, able to augment the waning autonomy and agency of states and shape the behavior of firms through her purchasing choices.[16]

---

16 Josée Johnston, "The Citizen-Consumer Hybrid: Ideological Tensions and the Case of Whole Foods Market," *Theory and Society* 37, 2007, 229–70; see also Josée Johnston, Andrew Biro, and Norah MacKendrick. "Lost in the Supermarket: The Corporate-Organic Foodscape and the Struggle for Food Democracy," *Antipode* 41: 3, 2009, 509–32.

However, lifestyle politics has not been accompanied by a clear idea about how consumers and their choices can save the planet. Some take a radical stance that eschews consumerism and calls for dramatically reducing consumption, particularly for wealthy Westerners. Others propose an ameliorative, middle-way approach that focuses on buying sustainably produced things rather than fewer things. In the United States, lifestyle politics is all the rage and both consumption messages are omnipresent. Minimalism is chic and restorative—thousands of people have embarked on Dave Bruno's "100 thing challenge," paring down their belongings to 100 items. People scrub their hands and souls with the "conscience clearing power" of J.R. Watkins natural soap. Graham Hill, an environmental entrepreneur, has developed a new line of luxury micro-apartments for urban dwellers. The 420-square-foot prototype debuted in 2012, complete with moving wall, telescoping coffee table ($3,325) and high-tech Murphy bed ($21,250) to save space. Hill argues that Americans of all socioeconomic backgrounds simply buy too much stuff. All this stuff puts us in debt, hurts the planet, and generally makes us unhappy. He encourages us to "clear the arteries of our lives" by downsizing our stuff to an "edited set of possessions" that reflect who we really are. "Small is sexy!" By experiencing the "joy of less" we can achieve happiness and heal the planet in the process.[17]

---

17   Graham Hill, TED Talk, 2013; Elizabeth Warren and Amelia Warren Tyagi have written a book challenging the veracity of American overspending. See *The Two-Income Trap: Why Middle-Class Parents Are Going Broke*, New York: Basic Books, 2004.

Nature, Capitalism, and the Entrepreneurial Spirit

Shopping at Whole Foods quenches this desire to clear the arteries of our lives. We can buy organic abate gretel pears from Argentina and Brillat-Savarin cheese from France and feel like good consumer-citizens knowing that our dollars are helping farm animals and poor women in the Global South. Yet while Mackey acknowledges the power of consumers, they are not the keystone in his conscious-capitalism model. The protagonist is himself, the entrepreneur:

> Entrepreneurs are the true heroes in a free-enterprise economy, driving progress in business, society, and the world. They solve problems by creatively envisioning different ways the world could and should be. With their imagination, creativity, passion, and energy, they are the greatest creators of widespread change in the world.[18]

The roots of Mackey's earth-friendly entrepreneurial vision and belief in holistic, free-market capitalism stretch back to the Physiocrats, eighteenth-century French philosophers who believed that markets were part of the natural order and followed natural laws just as living organisms did. For Mackey, a well-managed, conscious firm becomes "self-managing, self-motivating, self-organizing, and self-healing like any evolved, sentient being."[19] The expansion of capitalism to every nook and cranny of the planet is seen as an

18 Mackey and Sisodia, *Conscious Capitalism*, p. 14.
19 Ibid., p. 31.

organic process, stemming from humanity's "natural" inclination to truck, barter, and trade.

The story of markets and firms enmeshed with nature (and following the laws of nature) differs from liberal, Kantian notions of nature in which society is fundamentally separate from nature. While humanity's relationship with nature has changed over the centuries—from fear of its wildness, to nostalgia for it as "a place to go back to," and recently back to fear at the thought of destroying it—in the liberal framework, society always remains external or opposed to nature. This view, illustrated by NGO names like EarthFirst!, sees the firm, markets, and society as violating nature by their very existence, fouling its pristine, prehuman state.[20]

Mackey doesn't see markets and firms as alien forces violating nature and thinks that environmentalists need to "open their minds" and stop obsessing over "environmental Armageddon." In the conscious capitalism model, the environment is a stakeholder with rights equal to those of the investor, supplier, worker, customer, and community. The needs of the environment are built in to the business model, as demonstrated by Whole Foods practices such as ethical purchasing, LEED certification, waste reduction, and use of reusable packaging and nontoxic cleaning products. For Mackey, a smart entrepreneur running a conscious business isn't an external

---

20   Neil Smith, *Uneven Development: Nature, Capital, and the Production of Space*, Athens: University of Georgia Press, 2008, p. 69; see also Erik Swyngdeouw, "Impossible Sustainability and the Post-Political Condition," in David Gibbs and Rob Krueger, eds., *The Sustainable Development Paradox: Urban Political Economy in the United States and Europe*, New York: Guilford Press, 2007.

force damaging the planet. Instead, a conscious business "genuinely cares about the planet and all the sentient beings that live on it, . . . celebrates the glories of nature, [and] thinks beyond carbon and neutrality to become a healing force that nurses the ecosphere back to sustained vitality."[21]

Corporations have not always been friends to the environment (or people), as disasters like Bhopal, Love Canal, Brightwater Horizon, and the ongoing horror show of Shell Nigeria clearly demonstrate. Chronic, long-term environmental problems like water shortages and erosion are expected to become acute for many communities and countries in coming years. But Mackey is confident that as business continues to evolve to its next phase, conscious capitalism, it will be able to solve these problems because conscious entrepreneurs (like himself) have a "fundamentally more sophisticated and complex way of thinking" that derives from "high levels of analytical, emotional, and spiritual intelligence."[22] While we may be tempted to fix environmental problems by demanding restrictions on firms, Mackey urges us to hold back: when firms follow a conscious business model they are naturally in tune with the world around them—they are a sentient, symbiotic part of it.

Free Market Seductions

The free market story is appealing. It references values like freedom, creativity, and beauty and counterposes itself against

---

21   Mackey and Sisodia, *Conscious Capitalism*, pp. 151, 31.
22   Ibid., p. 31.

images of drudgery, dictatorship, and starvation. But the history of markets (and the firms that operate within them) is not a nature story.

Today, the dominant discourse governing discussion of markets, states, and companies is neoliberalism, and Mackey's free market business model and historical narrative fit neatly within this framework. In this vision, the economic sphere is "an autonomous, self-adjusting, and self-regulated system that [can] achieve a natural equilibrium spontaneously and produce increased wealth."[23] But the free market historical narrative lacks empirical weight. As economic historian Karl Polanyi argued decades ago, capitalist markets are a product of state engineering, not nature.[24]

The history of industrial development in the United States, often considered the epicenter of free markets, demonstrates the political nature of markets. The history of market formation in the United States reveals an industrial structure supplied by goods and capital extracted from slave labor and facilitated through a state-sponsored, genocidal land grab. Far-reaching government legislation protected domestic markets and infant industries from external competition, and federal and state governments played a central role in the development of physical infrastructure (canals, railways, telegraphy) and the creation of huge bodies of agricultural and industrial knowledge—all

23   Bernard E. Harcourt, *The Illusion of Free Markets: Punishment and the Myth of Natural Order*, Cambridge, MA: Harvard University Press, 2011.
24   Karl Polanyi, *The Great Transformation: The Political and Economic Origins of Our Times*, Boston: Beacon Press, 2001.

essential elements in the genesis of American industrial capitalism.

At the same time, society's greatest inventions and innovations of the past two hundred years—rockets to the moon, penicillin, computers, the internet—were not bestowed upon us by lone entrepreneurs and firms operating in free markets under conditions of healthy competition. They were the work of institutions: CERN and the Department of Defense created the internet, while Bell Labs—a subdivision of AT&T, freed from market competition by federally granted monopoly rights—generated transistors, radar, information theory, "quality control," and dozens of other innovations central to our epoch.[25] Nearly every advance in science, technology, and mathematics emerged from people working together at universities supported by government funding. Creativity and innovation come from many places. Companies produce influential innovations, but so do other institutions that operate outside the confines of the profit motive, competitive markets, and the bottom line.

As Cambridge professor of economics Ha-Joon Chang argues, this is neither theoretical quibbling nor simply a quest for historical "truth." Instead, getting the historical narrative right is important because the stories we tell "deeply affect the very way in which we understand the nature and the development of the market, as well as its interrelationship with the state

---

25   John Gertner, *The Idea Factory: Bell Labs and the Great Age of American Innovation*, New York: Penguin, 2013.

and other institutions."[26] In the neoliberal narrative states are interlopers, under the thumb of rent-seeking politicians and bureaucrats, whose field of action should be restricted. The market, and the firm within it, is a natural thing following nature's laws, and the state is an unnatural, potentially dangerous thing, following human laws. The implication of this historical narrative is that the state must always justify its actions—justify why it is messing with natural market processes that, according to neoliberals, don't need its intervention.

This is disingenuous: What this model does not specify is the type of state intervention it requires or presumes. Many neoliberals and libertarians (like Mackey) say the state should stick to protecting private property and people against crime, minimal infrastructure provision, and basic laws to protect society from people or companies who wish to break laws (like environmental and public health laws).[27] But there is no natural explanation for why these interventions are justified and others, like free higher education or single-payer healthcare, are not. Recent battles at World Trade Organization (WTO) meetings over child labor and toxic dumping, and whether banning them constituted justifiable state interventions, demonstrate just how historical and contestable is the relationship between the state and the market.[28] It is a *political*

26   Ha-Joon Chang, "Breaking the Mould: An Institutionalist Political Economy Alternative to the Neoliberal Theory of the Market and the State," United Nations Research Institute for Social Development, Social Policy and Development Programme Paper No. 6, 2001.
27   See the discussion of the carceral state in Harcourt, *The Illusion of Free Markets*.
28   See, for example, Ha-Joon Chang, *Kicking Away the Ladder: Development Strategy in Historical Perspective*, London: Anthem, 2003.

relationship, formed according to existing norms about rights and obligations that change over time and space.

Designating the market as natural and the state as unnatural is a convenient fiction for those wedded to the status quo. It makes the current distribution of power, wealth, and resources seem natural and thus inevitable and uncontestable. But of course this isn't true. States shape, sustain, and often create, markets, including neoliberal markets. The complexion of those markets depends on the balance of class forces at any given point in time. Capitalist markets, and the inequality and degradation they engender, are a political creation not a product of nature.[29] Nature and society (and states and markets) are inseparable—simultaneously produced by humans through ideological, political, and economic processes. Understanding this enables us to challenge the dominant idea of natural, free markets and the emancipatory potential of the firm promised by Mackey.

Saving the Planet

Fine. Free markets don't exist and other institutions like states clearly matter. But how are these other institutions going to stop global warming and rainforest destruction and species

---

29 Karl Marx made a similar point about the taken-for-granted class structure of society: "Nature does not produce on the one side owners of money or commodities and on the other men possessing nothing but their own labor-power. This relation has no natural basis, neither is its social base one that is common to all historical periods. It is clearly the result of a past historical development, the product of many economic revolutions, of the extinction of a whole series of older forms of social production," *Capital*, 1:169, quoted in Smith, *Uneven Development*, p. 69.

extinction? States, aside from the big players, appear weaker than ever (with less autonomy, power, authority), and their ability to tell corporations what to do is limited by their need for economic development and their membership in international bodies like the World Trade Organization that explicitly prohibit most environmental restrictions.

On the flip side, transnational corporations are stronger than ever. One giant company, like Unilever or Walmart, affects millions of people around the world every day through its global supply chains. Free markets don't exist, but maybe corporations are still the best, most sensible, way to heal the planet. They have reach, influence, and an unrivaled ability to coordinate action quickly. In Mackey's story an enlightened corporation with a positive mission that honors all its stakeholders can heal the planet. He says that a company can create a virtuous cycle of production and consumption that will stand the test of time if it treats its suppliers, its workers, and its community and the environment right.

Many companies like General Electric, Walmart, IKEA, SC Johnson, Pepsi, and Puma seem to be starting down the path of conscious capitalism, particularly in the adoption of sustainable, "eco-business" practices such as supply-chain tracing, auditing, green procurement, certification, eco-labeling, and life-cycle assessment to radically streamline their operations, reduce their waste, and raise profits. These eco-business practices improve the image of big corporations through "greenwashing."[30] But an even bigger part of their appeal stems

30   See William S. Laufer, "Social Accountability and Corporate Greenwashing," *Journal of Business Ethics* 43, 2003.

from their utility in helping companies gain control over their supply chains (which account for 60 to 90 percent of costs at big companies) in an increasingly competitive and uncertain global economy. More efficient and transparent supply chains allow companies to support the suppliers they like (and need) through logistical and financial support and dump the ones that produce shoddy, toxic products that cause embarrassment and lawsuits. Eco-business practices also boost profits that are then channeled into developing new, lower-cost products to compete in emerging markets and cutting costs on existing products for established, wealthier markets.[31]

At the same time that big companies are building in sustainable business practices, environmental NGOs (such as Greenpeace and the Sierra Club) are moving to embrace the eco-business model. The probusiness environmental message of the 1987 Brundtland Report, in combination with the weakened power of states to control the actions of corporations, have pushed big environmental NGOs to change their stance toward corporations over the past decade and to focus on the marketplace as the most viable lever of change.[32] As Gerald Butts, CEO of World Wildlife Fund Canada, explains about WWF's decision to partner with Coca-Cola:

We could spend fifty years lobbying seventy-five national governments to change the regulatory framework for the

31 Peter Dauvergne and Jane Lister, *Eco-Business: A Big-Brand Takeover of Sustainability,* Cambridge, Mass.: MIT Press, 2013.
32 *People and the Planet Report,* Report 01/12, London: Royal Society Science Policy Centre, 2012.

way these commodities are grown and produced. Or these folks at Coke could make a decision that they're not going to purchase anything that isn't grown or produced in a certain way—and the whole global supply chain changes overnight.[33]

Big environmental groups may criticize neoliberalism and transnational corporations, but these days their strategic agendas look very similar to those of companies like Whole Foods and Walmart. The state is viewed as a suspect, ineffective force, while the firm becomes the key vehicle for change.

In light of these global trends, doesn't it make sense to expand eco-business practices and scale up the Whole Foods model? If companies act consciously and responsibly, can we free ourselves from the vicious production and consumption cycles that currently exist and develop a healthier relationship with the planet? The Whole Foods model is, without a doubt, a better way of doing business than Walmart deploys. But despite its appeal, conscious capitalism is not a solution to the destructive impact of corporations or the environmental crisis on the horizon.

There are two interrelated problems with the model. First, it claims to produce virtuous growth that outsmarts and escapes the competitive tendencies of capitalism that are currently destroying the planet and impoverishing

---

33 Dauvergne and Lister, *Eco-Business*, pp. 19–20. Companies are benefiting from their partnerships with environmental groups as well. The Sierra Club logo on its Green Works line of products has enabled Clorox to capture 40 percent of the natural cleaning products market.

billions of people. Mackey's *central* argument is that his philosophy of capitalism is not dominated by broad imperatives, like profit and competition. David Harvey contends that competition is inescapable in capitalism: Firms must grow and generate profits in a system characterized by "the coercive laws of competition." Harvey notes: "If I, as a capitalist, do not reinvest in expansion and a rival does, then after a while I am likely to be driven out of business. I need to protect and expand my market share. I have to reinvest to stay a capitalist."[34] When many firms invest in the same thing competition gets fierce, and profits go down.

Mackey acknowledges that firms must make a profit, but brushes off the necessity of trade-offs, the centrality of the profit imperative, and the problems posed by competition. In his model profits arise naturally from innovation and the virtuous feedback loop of honoring stakeholders, and competition is thereby outsmarted.

If Whole Foods Market, for example, had to compete with Walmart strictly on the basis of supply chain efficiency or distribution economies of scale, it would be impossible for us to win. But what we can do is be more nimble, more creative, and more innovative and provide higher-quality service while creating a better store environment. By the time Walmart figures out what we are doing, we will have moved on to newer and better

34   David Harvey, *The Enigma of Capital: and the Crises of Capitalism*, New York: Oxford University Press, 2011, p. 43.

innovations that create new value for our ever-evolving customers."[35]

Mackey cites Raj Sisodia's *Firms of Endearment* study to show that over a fifteen-year period, twenty-eight conscious businesses outperformed the S&P 500 index by a factor of 10.5. The curious thing about Mackey's story though, is the dearth of *old* conscious firms. When he looks back in history he sees companies that were great for a while (General Motors, IBM, Kodak) and then failed or became less profitable. Mackey chalks this up to both the novelty of his entrepreneurial vision and his belief that the older companies simply lost their way, abandoned their core values, got greedy, lazy, etc. Many businesspeople have shared core elements of Mackey's business philosophy over the years. The fact that none of these principles has stood the test of time is indicative of the long-term effects of competition, not greed or laziness.

Whole Foods has prospered so far. No doubt this is related, in part, to the virtuous feedback loop it has established and the wealthy tranche of the population it supplies. But the company also has a rapacious appetite. It has bought and absorbed dozens of companies and hundreds of free-standing health food stores in its short life. It has grown from one store in 1980 to 373 stores today (with 107 more in the pipeline).[36]

---

35 Mackey and Sisodia, *Conscious Capitalism*, p. 80.
36 "Whole Foods Market Reports First Quarter Results, Outlook for Fiscal Year 2014," www.wholefoodsmarket.com/sites/default/files/media/Global/Company%20Info/PDFs/WFM-2014-Q1-financial.pdf.

This fact cannot be separated from its prosperity. Today it is the world's largest retailer of organic and natural foods. But its ability to maintain its monopoly is not unlimited. If we look at the decline of a firm like IBM, which once seemed invincible, whose workers were virtually guaranteed lifetime employment, good wages, and a decent place to work, the imperatives of profit and competition (and the shelf-life of monopoly powers) become clear. No matter how conscious or high-minded a business owner, if faced with a competitive market where profits are declining, her only choices are to abandon her principles or perish. Competition trumps philosophy every time.

Maybe Mackey has discovered a magic formula that will keep Whole Foods profitable for the long haul. If so, will the model still work? The answer is no. Even if, miraculously, all or most firms could maintain their principles, stay in business, and eke out profits through constant innovation, diversification, and creativity, the sum of all this activity is still an ever-expanding capitalist market, in which the environment always loses.

Ideas of conscious capitalism, sustainable capitalism, or eco-business all mask the essential need for firms to keep producing more. Moves by firms to improve relations with suppliers and reduce resource use and waste are *not* designed to slow down production and consumption. Eco-business practices are a way for firms to speed up growth, speed up their ability to enter new markets, gain new customers, and make more profits. As Stacey Mitchell, co-director of the Institute for Local Self-Reliance, argues:

Walmart is accelerating the cycle of consumption, speed-
ing up how fast products move from factory to shelf to
house to landfill. Even if Walmart does reduce the
resources used to make a T-shirt or a television set, those
gains will be more than outstripped by growth in the
number of T-shirts and TVs we're consuming. It's one
step forward and three steps back.[37]

Ultimately, Whole Foods operates within a capitalist world
economy in which firms must expand if they are to survive.
Sustainable business practices sustain the ability of firms to
exist and expand in an increasingly competitive, resource-
starved global economy. Eco-practices don't change the
nature of production, consumption, or disposal. They don't
decrease the ecological footprint of firms (or humans).
Sustainable practices enable firms to make bigger, deeper
footprints as they expand into new markets and tap new
sources of supply. As long as production is designed to
increase profits, as it must be in capitalism, rather than to
meet the needs of humans, the environment will never escape
and never be healed. As geographer Neil Smith argued: In
capitalism "nature becomes a *universal means of production* in
the sense that it not only provides the subjects, objects, and
instruments of production, but is also in its totality an append-
age to the production process."[38]

---

37   Stacy Mitchell, *Big-Box Swindle: The True Cost of Mega-Retailers
and the Fight for America's Independent Businesses*, Boston: Beacon Press,
2007, quoted in Dauvergne and Lister, *Eco-Business*, p. 23.
38   Smith, *Uneven Development*, p. 71 (emphasis in original).

Competition is a defining feature of capitalism, one that will eventually steamroll all warm, fuzzy versions of capitalism, and even if long-term, virtuous growth were possible, the imperatives of the profit motive require that capitalism keep expanding and growing, consuming and destroying the planet as it goes. Sustainable production and eco-business practices do absolutely nothing to challenge this maxim.

This leads to the second problem with the model, which is that it relies on the notion that all stakeholders can be honored equally. This is, quite simply, not possible within capitalism. Consumers and investors must always be prioritized over the environment and over workers. The firm is not a democratic institution, and it can't be the centerpiece of a radical project for environmental justice.

In Mackey's framework the market is the central organizing institution and relations of exchange are what bind people together. He believes that in a competitive market, these relations of exchange are always benevolent because they are "based on the principles of equality and freedom." Investors trade their money for more money and workers trade their ability to work for a wage to buy the things they need. "No matter how large a business becomes, it never acquires coercive power over customers, team members, or other stakeholders. All the business can do is offer each of its stakeholders a menu of choices; the stakeholders have the freedom to choose."[39]

But as Marx argued, even though workers and investors meet each other in the marketplace, they do not confront each

---

39   Mackey and Sisodia, *Conscious Capitalism*, p. 165.

other as equals. Focusing on processes of exchange hides the class basis of society. Workers are free to sell their ability to work for a wage, but history has also "freed" them from owning the means to support themselves in any other way.

Mackey in fact understands this. He never says that all stakeholders should be equal. Instead, he maintains that conscious capitalism "optimizes value" for all stakeholders— meaning to make it as good as possible within the system or structure of relationships in place. But optimizing gains for stakeholders in capitalism has built-in limits: some stakeholders, like investors, will always have much more power than other stakeholders, like workers. Mackey claims this is necessary because investors are paid last, and without that power, the stockholders will inevitably be exploited by management or some other stakeholder of the business.

Whole Foods workers are better off than many retail and fast food workers.[40] Permanent, full-time employees earn considerably more than minimum wage, and both part-time and full-time workers receive health insurance: part-timers working at least twenty hours a week can buy full-cost coverage after working 400 hours, and full-timers can get lower-cost coverage after working 800 hours. Executive pay is kept in check, relative to other major corporations, and the

---

40   The benefits enjoyed by Whole Foods workers do not extend up the supply chain. A June 2014 *Forbes* article revealed that Whole Foods sells tilapia and artisanal cheese produced by prisoners earning a base pay of 60 cents a day: Jennifer Alsever, "Prison Labor's New Frontier: Artisanal Foods," *Fortune*, June 2, 2014. The current nostalgia for, and fetishization of, farmers markets, local produce, and mothers cooking slow food for their families, popularized by writers like Michael Pollen, also ignores the exploitation and invisibility suffered by farmworkers toiling in the US and elsewhere.

management structure is more horizontal than vertical. However, wages for many Whole Foods employees fall far below a living wage. Cashier wages range between $8 an hour to $14 for permanent employees, while workers in other parts of the store make between $10 and $15 an hour. Despite its claims that Whole Foods honors all stakeholders, many team members, including full-time workers, are forced to rely on food stamps, and a recent study found that 17 percent of Whole Food's Massachusetts employees are enrolled in Medicaid.[41] The company's "gainsharing" program bumps up this pay rate for some workers, but bonuses and promotions are contingent on competition between workers: teams compete against other in-store teams, and stores and regions compete against each other, on benchmarks including profitability and customer service.

In July 2013, Chicago Whole Foods workers joined striking fast food and retail workers in the Fight for $15 campaign, demanding a living wage, an end to the points system (workers who commit infractions, such as calling in sick, collect penalty points that can lead to termination), and the right to unionize. Mackey has expressed ambivalence toward unions on numerous occasions, memorably likening them to having herpes: "The union is like having herpes. It doesn't kill you, but it's unpleasant and inconvenient."[42] Whole Foods, Starbucks, and Costco were vocal opponents of the Employee

---

41 Stacy Mitchell, "New Data Show How Big Chains Free Ride on Taxpayers at the Expense of Responsible Small Businesses," ILSR.org, June 7, 2013.

42 Nick Paumgarten, "Food Fighter: Does Whole Foods' CEO Know What's Best for You?" *New Yorker*, January 4, 2010.

Free Choice Act, proposing a "third way" option that preserved the employer-dominated secret ballot system. Lobbying against the bill, Mackey declared that card-check neutrality "violates a bedrock principle of American democracy."[43] At stores where union murmurings occur, workers report being forced to attend "Union Awareness Training" meetings to warn them against the dangers of union "infiltration."[44] A 2009 investigation by *Mother Jones* found that Whole Foods managers threatened workers at closed-door meetings with losing their benefits if they voted for a union. According to the investigation, one of Whole Foods' "six strategic goals" for 2013, as outlined in company documents, was to remain "100 percent union free."[45]

It's worth remembering that, while the slightly better pay, benefits, and working conditions enjoyed by Whole Foods workers seem rare in today's job market, this wasn't the case just a few decades ago, when many unionized supermarket chains offered decent livelihoods to their workers. The Whole Foods model is better than Walmart, but it's hardly a utopian vision. It is not democratic and is in no way defined by equitable power relations. As Mackey claims, workers are offered a "menu" of choices. The menu is decided by him and Whole Foods investors. When profits decline or competition increases, as they tend to do in capitalism, workers are at the

43   Alec MacGillis, "Executives Lay Out Compromise to 'Card Check' Labor Bill," *Washington Post*, March 22, 2009.

44   Sharon Smith, "Something Stinks at Whole Foods," *Counterpunch*, May 8, 2009.

45   Josh Harkinson, "Are Starbucks and Whole Foods Union Busters?" motherjones.com, April 6, 2009.

whim of the company, just like workers at any other company. If team members don't like it, they are free to work elsewhere. But in a system where workers have no other means to support themselves without a wage, the freedom to work elsewhere is not much freedom at all.

Environmental Justice Needs Radical, Democratic Institutions

Conscious capitalism, while attractive in some respects, is not a solution to the environmental and social degradation that accompanies the system of for-profit production. The "coercive laws of competition" are inescapable in capitalism, which means that conscious business philosophies will be short-lived. More important, even sustainable production in a for-profit system will consume and destroy the planet's resources. Sustainable business practices are designed to make global production easier and more profitable for companies in an increasingly competitive global environment. While they make consumers feel good and improve efficiency and waste at the unit level, eco-practices don't slow down production and consumption at the systemic level. They speed up these processes, devouring resources at an ever-expanding rate.

The widespread popularity of ethical consumption and lifestyle politics is a clear indication that people care about the environment and don't want to destroy the planet. But the firm can't be the driver of a radical project to reduce humanity's ecological footprint. Firms are not democratic institutions, and they cannot escape the imperatives of capitalism. When consumers and environmental NGOs channel their desire for environmental justice through the firm, their desires get absorbed into business strategies for growth and expansion. By focusing on the firm, we legitimate its centrality and the entire for-profit production architecture.

Society must decide what kind of world it wants to live in, and these decisions must be made through democratic structures and processes. Buying better things is not a substitute for the hard *political* choices that societies need to make about limiting consumption and resource use, and finding a replacement for the psychological crutch of consumerism. States seem toothless in the face of environmental degradation, but they are not inherently weak. They simply represent the existing balance of class forces. If we don't want to live in an environmental wasteland, we must build up democratic institutions to organize production and consumption around the needs of humans, not the needs of capital.

3

The Oracle of O: Oprah and the Neoliberal Subject

In the Oprah Winfrey lore, one particular story is repeated over and over. When Oprah was seventeen she won the Miss Fire Prevention Contest in Nashville, Tennessee. Until that year every winner had had a mane of red hair, but Oprah would prove to be a game changer. When asked what she wanted to be when she grew up she replied, "I would like to be a journalist. I would like to tell other people's stories in a way that makes a difference in their lives and the world."[1] This vignette is recounted for two reasons. It enables us to imagine the moment when Oprah first stepped onto the path to becoming a media mogul and household name. (She is so omnipresent that we refer to her simply as Oprah.) It also demonstrates the wonder of Oprah—that a poor, black girl could win a beauty contest for white girls in 1971 in the Deep South is a testament to her greatness.

The contest was the first of many successes for Oprah. She has won numerous Emmys, has been nominated for an

---

1   Oprah Winfrey, Harvard commencement speech, May 30, 2013.

Oscar, and appears regularly on magazine lists like *Time*'s 100 Most Influential People. In 2013 she was awarded the Presidential Medal of Freedom and named the Most Powerful Celebrity in the United States by *Forbes*. Oprah founded the Oprah Book Club, which is often credited with reviving Americans' interest in reading, and in 2011 started her own television network, the Oprah Winfrey Network (OWN).

Oprah's generosity and philanthropic spirit is legendary. During the *Oprah Winfrey Show*'s twenty-five-season run she showered her studio audiences with gifts (like cars), gave her guests extravagant makeovers and vacations, and rewarded dedicated employees with cash, cars, and jewelry. She started philanthropic projects like the Angel Network, which built fifty-five schools in twelve countries and restored hundreds of homes following Hurricanes Katrina and Rita.

Oprah's philanthropic reach extends beyond the United States to Africa. In 2007 she opened the Oprah Winfrey Leadership Academy for Girls, a posh boarding school for poor South African girls. Oprah provides the girls with a top-tier education and then pays their college expenses. She also contributes millions of dollars to other nonprofits through the Oprah Winfrey Foundation. More recently, Oprah teamed up with Bono in the Red Campaign to raise money for the Global Fund to Fight AIDS, Tuberculosis and Malaria.

Oprah has legions of obsessive, devoted fans who write her letters and follow her into public restrooms. Oprah basks in their love: "I know people really, really, really *love* me, *love* me." And she loves them right back. It's part of her "higher calling." Oprah believes that she was put on this earth to lift people up, to help them "live their best life."

"I'm very clear about what my purpose on Earth is," she said. "The work I do on television is just a way of me manifesting myself as a vessel and a vehicle for the larger energy [and universal purpose] I call God."[2]

Oprah's stories encourage people to love themselves, believe in themselves, and follow their dreams. Even presidents are inspired. When Obama conferred the Medal of Honor on Oprah he said, "Oprah's greatest strength has always been her ability to help us discover the best in ourselves."[3] Oprah's success and charisma undergird her core message that anything is possible. Her story is a real-life, rags-to-riches tale that inspires a belief that wealth and success are achievable if we open our minds. She tells us over and again that "the boundaries and limitations that prevent us from living our Utopia are those we have created in our own mind and have made a part of our own reality."[4]

It's a Cold World Out There

Oprah's popularity stems in part from her message of empathy, support, and love in an increasingly stressful,

---

2   Janet Lowe, *Oprah Winfrey Speaks: Insight from the World's Most Influential Voice*, New York: Wiley, 1998; Oprah Winfrey interview with Moira Forbes, "A Conversation with Oprah winfrey," www.youtube.com, September 18, 2012.

3   "Remarks by the President at the Presidential Medal of Freedom Ceremony," Whitehose.gov, November 20, 2003.

4   Janice Peck, *The Age of Oprah: Cultural Icon for the Neoliberal Era*, Boulder, CO: Paradigm, 2008, p. 110.

alienating society. Three decades of companies restructuring their operations by eliminating jobs (through attrition, technology, and outsourcing) and dismantling both organized labor and the welfare state has left workers in an extremely precarious situation. Today, new working-class jobs are primarily low-wage service jobs, and the perks that once went along with middle-of-the-road white-collar jobs have disappeared. Flexible, project-oriented, contingent work has become the norm, enabling companies to ratchet up their requirements for all workers except those at the very top (jobs that in the past required only a high school education now require a college degree). Meanwhile, the costs of education, housing, childcare, and health care have skyrocketed, making it yet more difficult for individuals and households to get by, never mind prosper.

The situation is bleak: over 60 percent of the jobs lost during the Great Recession were good jobs, middle-income jobs. The average unemployed person spent forty weeks on the unemployment rolls in 2012, and today there are more than four people vying for every job opening. In the corporate world, job openings elicit hundreds of résumés, and when foreign automakers open plants in the US South tens of thousands apply. A third of households have negative wealth or no assets, and three-fourths have less than six months' income in savings. One in three people say that if they lost their job they wouldn't be able to make their mortgage or rent payment within one month.[5]

---

5   Rapoport and Wheary, *Where the Poor and the Middle Class Meet.*

While the working poor grew used to crushed dreams a long time ago, the emotional toll of the recent crisis on the middle class is stark. The *New York Times* recently reported that the US middle class is no longer the most affluent in the world: even economic self-help guru Suze Orman tells older middle-class people that they'll need to work until at least age seventy and "live below their means" if they're going to make enough to support themselves through their retirement. But older workers, particularly those who lost their jobs in the recession, are finding it difficult to get, or stay, hired. Psychologists say that Millennials are the most stressed-out generation ever, set loose in a society that tells them the sky's the limit, but that also sets requirements for, and expectations of, success sky-high. Meanwhile, 45 percent of the unemployed are young people. Suicide is now the second leading cause of death among college students, and the leading cause of death, after cancer and heart disease, among male baby boomers.

Finding the Sweet Life

In this climate of stress and uncertainty, Oprah tells us the stories of her life to help us understand our feelings, cope with difficulty, and improve our lives. She presents her personal journey and metamorphosis from a poor little girl in rural Mississippi to a billionaire prophet as a model for overcoming adversity and finding "a sweet life."[6]

---

6   Oprah Winfrey, Spelman College commencement speech, April 19, 2012.

Oprah's wildly successful trajectory frequently draws comparisons to the Horatio Alger myth. She even won the Horatio Alger Award, which honors public figures who have overcome adversity and are passionate about supporting education. At first glance, Oprah seems to embody that myth. Starbucks offers Oprah Chai Tea to benefit the Oprah Winfrey Leadership Foundation, and on one of many trips to Africa Oprah told a group of impoverished children who had been orphaned by the HIV/AIDS epidemic that with hard work and determination they too could be like her one day: "I grew up like many of you. No running water. No electricity, as a little girl. You can overcome poverty and despair in your life with an education. I am living proof of that."[7]

Horatio Alger, a sensitive Harvard alum, was horrified by the ills of industrial capitalism in New York City during the late nineteenth century. In response, he wrote a hundred inspirational novels about young men who escaped poverty and achieved success, idealizing a time when "honesty, thrift, self-reliance, industry, a cheerful whistle, and an open, manly face" were all it took to achieve the American Dream. The Alger stories had fallen out of favor by the turn of the century, not because they sported titles like *Ragged Dick*, but because critics like H.L. Mencken thought that Alger was deluded about what it takes to succeed in America. Mark Twain was

---

7   Heather Laine Talley and Monica J. Casper, "Oprah Goes to Africa: Philanthropic Consumption and Political (Dis)Engagement," in Trystan T. Cotten and Kimberly Springer, eds., *Stories of Oprah: The Oprahfication of American Culture*, Oxford: University of Mississippi Press, 2009.

also not a fan. He wrote an Alger parody about a "good little boy" named Jacob Blivens whose piousness couldn't save him from being turned into a "human nitro-glycerin rocket," body parts hurled across four townships. "You never saw a boy scattered so."[8]

Yet despite frequent comparisons to the Alger myth and its revived popularity, Oprah's story bears little resemblance to Alger's stories. His heroes never became extravagantly wealthy—success for Alger's plucky protagonists meant reaching the middle class and securing a steady job. Prosperity also depended heavily on a stroke of good luck (like saving a rich girl from being flattened by a falling safe) and earning the favor of a rich, kindly benefactor.[9] Conversely, Oprah credits her success in life to "being excellent" at everything she does and drawing strength from God and spirituality. Echoing the remedy of Rhonda Byrne (author of *The Secret*) for a hard-knocks life, Oprah attributes her billions to getting back what she puts out into the universe:

> What I recognize now is that my choice to, in every way, in every example, in every experience, do the right thing and the excellent thing, is what has created the brand . . . So doing the right thing, even when nobody knows you're doing the right thing, will always bring the right thing to you. I promise you that. Why? Because the third law of

8   Clifton Fadiman, "Party of One," *Holiday*, February 6, 1957, quoted in Richard Weiss, *The American Myth of Success: From Horatio Alger to Norman Vincent* Peale, New York: Basic Books, 1969; Mark Twain, *The Story of the Good Little Boy*, 1875.

9   Weiss, *American Myth*.

motion is always at work. For every action there is an equal and opposite reaction.[10]

This makes Oprah a much more exciting character to emulate. In her story, success comes from righteousness and hard work, not luck—so anyone can achieve it.

Oprah's biographical tale has been managed, mulled over, and mauled in the public gaze for thirty years and is a story familiar to millions of Americans. She used her precocious intelligence and wit to channel the pain of abuse and poverty into building an empire. She was on television by the age of nineteen and had her own show within a decade. The 1970s feminist movement opened the door to the domestic, private sphere, and the show walked in a decade later, breaking new ground as a public space to discuss personal troubles affecting Americans, particularly women. Oprah broached topics (divorce, depression, alcoholism, child abuse, adultery, incest) that had never before been discussed with such candor and empathy on television. The *Oprah Winfrey Show* was the top program in its time slot for twenty-five seasons.

The show's evolution over the decades mirrored the evolution of Oprah's own life. In its early years the show followed a "recovery model" in which guests and viewers were encouraged to overcome their problems through self-esteem building and learning to love themselves. Oprah herself was a part of the healing, both as sympathetic ear and as victim. She talked about expunging her "slave mentality" and famously

10   Winfrey, Spelman commencement speech.

admitted to drug use and childhood trauma in spontaneous, on-air confessions that shocked the world and endeared her to millions. But as copycat shows and criticisms of "trash talk" increased in the early 1990s, Oprah changed the show's format.

In 1994, Oprah declared that she was done with "victimization" and negativity: "It's time to move on from 'We are dysfunctional' to 'What are we going to do about it?'" Oprah credited her decision to her own personal evolution: "People must grow and change" or "they will shrivel up" and "their souls will shrink." In an appearance on *Larry King Live*, Oprah admitted that she had become concerned about the message of her show and so had decided to embark on a new mission "to lift people up." Themes of spirituality and empowerment displaced themes of personal pathology. For Oprah the transformation was total: "Today I try to do well and be well with everyone I reach or encounter. I make sure to use my life for that which can be of goodwill. Yes, this has brought me great wealth. More important, it has fortified me spiritually and emotionally."[11]

An episode with Marianne Williamson (a spiritual/self-help guru made famous by Oprah) demonstrated the transformation of the show and Oprah's worldview. The show featured a depressed, unhappy mother on welfare. Williamson encouraged her guest to let go of her "victim mentality," embrace the idea that "I have within me the power to break

---

11   Peck, *Age of Oprah*; Eva Illouz, *Oprah Winfrey and the Glamour of Misery: An Essay on Popular Culture*, Columbia University Press, 2003; *O, The Oprah Magazine*, "What I Know For Sure," May/June 2000.

through these constrictions," and realize that God is more powerful than welfare or depression. A different episode featured a young, single-mother named Clarissa who had recently lost her job, but who, after seeing an episode of *Oprah*, realized that instead of anger she should feel gratitude for being fired. According to Oprah, "Any time you get fired, you should say thank you," because "it obviously means you're not supposed to be there." Now that Clarissa was able to focus on "gratitude" rather than anger at losing her job, she could find her true calling in life and use her newfound freedom to go back to school. Oprah says that "opportunities, relationships, even money flowed [her] way when [she] learned to be grateful no matter what happened in [her] life."[12]

A stream of self-help gurus like Williamson, Rhonda Byrne, Eckhart Tolle, John Gray, Suze Orman, Deepak Chopra, and Sara Ban Breathnach have spent time on Oprah's stage over the past decade and a half, all with the same message. You have choices in life. External conditions don't determine your life. You do. It's all inside you, in your head, in your wishes and desires. Thoughts are destiny, so thinking positive thoughts will enable positive things to happen.

Oprah channels the message of the gurus through her own story, having learned that everything in life happens for a reason, including failure. "Failure is just a way for our lives to show us we're moving in the wrong direction, that we should try something different." When bad things happen to

12   Peck, *Age of Oprah*, pp. 130, 220; *The Best of Oprah's What I Know for Sure*, Supplement to *O, The Oprah Magazine*, Nov 2000.

us, it's because we're drawing them toward us with unhealthy thinking and behaviors. "Don't complain about what you don't have. Use what you've got. To do less than your best is a sin. Every single one of us has the power for greatness because greatness is determined by service—to yourself and others." If we listen to that quiet "whisper" and fine-tune our "internal, moral, emotional GPS" we too can learn the secret of success.[13]

Neoliberalism and the "Mind Cure"

Janice Peck, in her work as professor of journalism and communication studies, has studied Oprah for years. She argues that to understand the Oprah phenomenon we must return to the ideas swirling around in the Gilded Age, particularly in the fields of psychology and religion. The therapeutic/religious movements popular then, variously called "mind cure," "New Thought," etc., drew on the teachings of psychology to link societal problems with individual behavior, seeing both society's problems *and* their solutions as originating in individuals. In a time of social turmoil, the movements provided a path to "personal and societal wellbeing" that originated within the self. Practitioners argued that anyone could achieve self-actualization and success if they liberated their true, beautiful, inner selves and realized that the "material conditions of the world" don't control

13   *The Best of Oprah's What I Know for Sure*, Supplement to *O, The Oprah Magazine,* February 2001; Lowe, *Oprah Winfrey Speaks*, p. 167; Winfrey, Harvard commencement speech.

individual lives. Peck sees strong parallels in the mind-cure movement in the Gilded Age and Oprah's evolving enterprise in the New Gilded Age, the era of neoliberalism. She argues that Oprah's evolution from pathologizing problems to spiriting them away is mirrored in the evolution of neoliberalism starting in the 1980s.[14]

Many scholars have characterized neoliberalism as a class project, designed to rebuild the class power and wealth of the elite in US society following the economic, political, and social turmoil of the 1960 and 1970s. Neoliberal restructuring entailed both a political-economic dimension in the reorganization of laws and practices and an ideological dimension in which social issues were transformed into personal troubles. The locus of attention in neoliberalism became the self: we are all independent, autonomous actors meeting in the marketplace, making our destinies and in the process making society. The power of structural forces like capitalism to create inequality and limit life choices is downplayed or ignored, particularly among younger people.

Peck argues that Oprah's enterprise reinforces this neoliberal focus on the self: Oprah's "enterprise [is] an ensemble of ideological practices that help legitimize a world of growing inequality and shrinking possibilities by promoting and embodying a configuration of self compatible with that world." Nothing captures this ensemble of ideological practices better than *O Magazine*, whose aim is to "help women see every experience and challenge as an opportunity to grow

---

14   Peck, *Age of Oprah*, pp. 25, 32.

and discover their best self. To convince women that the real goal is becoming more of who they really are. To embrace their life."[15] *O Magazine* implicitly, and sometimes explicitly, identifies a range of problems in neoliberal capitalism and suggests ways for readers to adapt themselves to mitigate or overcome these problems.

Does your sixty-hour-a-week desk job make your back hurt and leave you emotionally exhausted and stressed? Of course it does. Studies show that "death by office job" is real—people who sit at a desk all day are more likely to be obese, depressed, or just dead for no discernible reason. But you can dull these effects and improve your wellness with these *O*-approved strategies: Become more of an "out-of-the-box thinker" because creative people are healthier. Bring photos, posters, and "kitschy figurines" to decorate your workspace—"you'll feel less emotionally exhausted and reduce burnout." Write down three positive things that happened during your workday every night before leaving the office to "reduce stress and physical pain from work."[16]

Even outside the workplace, stress is a constant in many people's lives today. To alleviate these feelings, meditation expert and psychotherapist Tara Brach recommends that when you're feeling stressed "notice what's going on inside of you, and mentally whisper *yes* to the experience; *yes* to the anxiety, *yes* to the tension, *yes* to the irritation. With each yes,

---

15   Peck, *Age of Oprah*, p. 217; *O, The Oprah Magazine* Facebook page, www.facebook.com/oprahmagazine/info.

16   *O, The Oprah Magazine*, January 2014.

you give space for the experience to unfold. Letting your feelings progress to their logical conclusion helps them dissolve." Remember what spiritual teacher and best-selling author Eckhart Tolle says: "We are not our thoughts. We are the awareness of our thoughts, disguised as people."[17]

In December 2013, *O* devoted a whole issue to anxiety and worry. The issue "conquers a lifetime's worth of anxieties and apprehensions," an apt subject given rising levels of anxiety across the age spectrum. In the issue, bibliotherapists Ella Berthoud and Susan Elderkin present a list of books for the anxious, prescribing them instead of a "trip to the pharmacy." Feeling claustrophobic because you're too poor to move out of your parent's house? Read *Little House on the Prairie*. Feeling stressed because your current project at work is ending and you don't have another lined up? Read *The Man Who Planted Trees*. Worried that you won't be able to pay the rent because you just lost your job? Read *The Wind-Up Bird Chronicles*. "Instead of feeling depressed, follow the lead hero Toru Okada, who, while jobless, embarks on a fantastic liberating journey that changes the way he thinks."[18]

If you're still feeling anxious, remember "that you can't control the job market, but you can shore up your future prospects by networking." And stop comparing yourself with other, more successful people. Instead, Nilofer Merchant (Silicon Valley corporate director and speaker) advises you to "try to harness your 'onlyness'": "Admire your own kick-ass

---

17   *O, The Oprah Magazine*, February 2014.
18   *O, The Oprah Magazine*, December 2013.

individuality" and don't engage in "comparisonitis" or "you'll miss your true value."[19]

Keep the inspiration flowing by putting one of *O Magazine*'s card-stock "quotables" up on the fridge, like this Kurt Vonnegut gem: "Of all the words of mice and men, the saddest are, 'it might have been.'" Not a Vonnegut fan? Flip the card over. On the back is a Wholly Guacamole advertisement reminding you to "start your day off on the guac foot!"[20]

The ads in *O* are the other half of the feel-good formula. Fill up that hole inside you with spirituality and really nice stuff. In the special issue on anxiety, the nine-page feature story on "how to worry productively" is followed by a ten-page segment on boots and a seven-page spread on makeup. *O* tells us what to buy to "live our best life" in the *O* list of "must-haves." Rain getting you down? Buy some cheeky ($168) rain boots because "the wrong footwear makes bad weather even gloomier." There's even a special "Why It's Worth It" section in each issue, explaining why you should buy things like a $250 Anne Fontaine "timeless button-down" shirt. (After five years it will cost you only $1 per wear!) Oprah's personal journey finds its way here as well: "I remember when I finally had enough money to splurge, I went out and bought a stack of Ralph Lauren towels. I still remember how soft they felt."[21]

Spirituality, self-actualization, and stuff are inseparable. Including the pages in which *O* presents readers with

---

19   Ibid.
20   *O, The Oprah Magazine*, January 2014.
21   *O, The Oprah Magazine*, December 2013.

Oprah-approved products, 70 percent of the anxiety issue is advertising. There's no contradiction here, though, because, as Oprah says, God is abundance:

> God—however you define or refer to Him, Her, or It—is for us. The forces of nature are for us, offering us life in abundance. Every day and every breath is magic—if we can only see it for what it is . . . I'm still trying to wrap my head around the idea that the little girl from Mississippi who grew up holding her nose in an outhouse now flies on her own plane—my own plane!—to Africa to help girls who grew up like her. *Amazing grace, how sweet the sound!* [22]

Oprah recognizes the pervasiveness of anxiety and alienation in our society. But instead of examining the economic or political basis of these feelings, she advises us to turn our gaze inward and reconfigure ourselves to become more adaptable to the vagaries and stresses of the neoliberal moment.

Not Just for Housewives

Oprah's reach extends beyond the maligned imaginary of housewives who spend their days going to spinning classes, helicopter parenting, writing in their gratitude journals, and popping Lexapro. Sociologist Heather Laine Talley and Monica Casper, head of the Department of Gender and

---

22   *O, The Oprah Magazine*, January 2014.

Women's Studies at the University of Arizona, argue that "*all* Americans consume Oprah whether they realize it or not."[23]

In her Cotton Mather meets Norman Vincent Peale commencement speeches, Oprah exhorts students at Stanford, Duke, Spelman, Howard, and Harvard to follow her example:

> When you're doing work you're meant to do, it feels right and every day is a bonus, regardless of what you're getting paid . . . So, I say to you, forget about the fast lane. If you really want to fly, just harness your power to your passion. Honor your calling. Everyone has one. Trust your heart and success will come to you.[24]

Millennials have internalized this message: A recent study found that young people believe that adulthood "should be a journey toward happiness and fulfillment, meaning and purpose, [and] self-actualization," one "marked by continuous development, discovery and growth."[25] Identity and

---

23　Tally and Casper, "Oprah Goes to Africa."

24　Oprah Winfrey, Stanford University commencement speech, June 15, 2008.

25　Douglas Hartmann and Teresa Toguchi Swartz, "The New Adulthood? The Transition to Adulthood from the Perspective of Transitioning Young Adults." in *Constructing Adulthood: Agency and Subjectivity in the Life Course. Advances in Life Course Research*, Vol. 10, edited by R. Macmillan, Oxford, 2007, quoted in Jennifer M. Silva, "Constructing Adulthood in an Age of Uncertainty," *American Sociological Review* 77: 4, 2012, 508; see also Anthony Giddens, *Modernity and Self-Identity: Self and Society in the Late Modern Age*, New York: Polity Press, 1991.

work are inseparable in this equation, not because people identify themselves by their occupation, but because more and more of our lives are spent working, networking, and building up our personal brand. We spend years acquiring social capital (connections, access to networks) and cultural capital (skills and education) so we can find a job we love and hopefully keep a roof over our heads.

The "do what you love" message is at the heart of the work-identity fusion. It advises you to follow your passion. If you're unhappy, it's because you're not following your passion. If your job sucks, you're at the wrong job. Video blogger and social media guru Gary Vaynerchuk's famous TED Talk is a "shot in the arm" for those pining for a more fulfilling life:

> There are way too many people in this room right now that are doing stuff they hate. Please stop doing that. There is no reason in 2008 to do shit you hate! None. Promise me you won't . . . Look yourself in the mirror and ask yourself, 'What do I want to do every day for the rest of my life?' Do that! I promise you can monetize that shit . . . Whatever you need to do, do it . . . Stop crying and keep hustling. 'Hustle' is the most important word ever. And that's what you need to do. You need to work so hard.[26]

The message is that if you make the right choices and build up enough social and cultural capital you can achieve personal

---

26   Gary Vaynerchuk, TED Talk, Web. 2.0 Expo, September 2008.

and professional success simultaneously in a virtuous cycle that reproduces itself (with constant exertion). Marie Forleo, another internet success story, embodies the virtuous cycle. Forleo is a bestselling author and creator of MarieTV, and she rubs elbows with Russell Simmons, Sir Richard Branson, Marianne Williamson, and, of course, Oprah. In a recent interview with *Forbes*, Forleo says that "outrageous success comes from thinking different, being different and having the confidence to always do what feels right in your heart."[27] She sells an eight-week online entrepreneurship course ($1,999) that promises to help you "create a business and a life you love." Forleo's business school, or "B-school" (formerly the Rich, Happy, and Hot B-School), teaches students how to market themselves, tap into social networks, build a web presence, and be happy in their personal lives. The school's motto is that you can "get anything you want. It doesn't take talent or luck to succeed. You just have to decide."[28]

Passion isn't easy, though. Happiness and career success are only for the serious. You have to be willing to put in some serious "sweat equity" and be ready for competition. If you reach the top and there is no one left to compete with, compete with yourself. As Oprah says: "At first I was nervous about the competition and then I became my own competition, raising the bar every year, pushing, pushing, pushing myself as hard as I knew."[29] You must be willing to work harder than

---

27 Dan Schwabel, "Marie Forleo: How She Grew Her Brand to Oprah Status," *Forbes*, May 16, 2013.

28 See www.marieforleo.com/.

29 Oprah Winfrey, Harvard commencement speech.

everyone else. In *O Magazine,* Suze Orman tells Nadia, a twenty-five-year-old freelancer who works at NPR and two other jobs but is still unable to make ends meet, that she must "be willing to do anything and everything asked of her" because "there are no guarantees."[30]

It's certainly true that there are no guarantees. It can be hard to get a leg up when everyone around you is trying to do the same thing. In a society organized around the profit motive, the effects get weird fast, as demonstrated by the vast sea of unpaid "educational" internships. Every college student (who can afford it) is encouraged to build connections and skills through internships, and competition for them is fierce. Columnist Madeleine Schwartz notes that interns are regularly encouraged to be "flexible," "energetic," "creative," and, most important, thankful for the opportunity to work for nothing.[31] The National Labor Relations Board recently stepped in after widespread exploitation of interns was brought to light. In 2011, Fox Searchlight Pictures was charged with violating the Fair Labor Standards Act, and since then similar lawsuits have been filed against other companies, including Warner Music Group, Atlantic Music, and publishing houses Condé Nast and Hearst Corporation. In October 2014, NBC Universal settled a class-action lawsuit brought by a group of its interns for $4.6 million.

Following your passion and doing what you love may also require you to forgo job stability and long-term employment

---

30 *O, The Oprah Magazine,* March 2014.
31 Madeleine Schwartz, "Opportunity Costs: The True Price of Internships," *Dissent,* Winter 2013.

on the always changing, always moving road to self-actualization. But job stability is rare these days: The average Millennial spends only 2.6 years at a company today. Some 30 percent of the US workforce is contingent labor, and by some estimates, 40 to 50 percent of jobs that produce an income will be organized as short-term, contract work by 2020. Career lifespans are lengthening to fifty or more years, so essentially half of Millennials can expect to be freelancers for their entire adult lives.[32]

In response to these dramatic shifts in the labor market, groups like the Freelancers Union have emerged. The Freelancers Union (formerly Working Today) was founded by Sarah Horowitz in 2001 and represents almost a quarter-million freelancers: writers, photographers, web designers, and other hard-up creative class comrades. Horowitz was named one of the 30 Top Social Entrepreneurs by *Forbes* and a Top 25 Most Promising Social Entrepreneur by *Businessweek*. The Freelancers Union offers health and pension insurance to qualified members, has successfully fought to reduce taxes on freelancers, and has introduced legislation to protect freelancers from deadbeat clients.[33]

In its focus on self-adjustment, gratitude, and service, the strategy presented by the Freelancers Union echoes Oprah's message. The union's website offers tips for branding yourself (be likable, tell a story, be personal, be memorable). It urges freelancers to think of building social

---

32   Mark Babbitt, "25 Jobs in a 50-Year Career: Is Gen Y Ready?" *Savvy Intern*, October 9, 2013.
33   See www.freelancersunion.org.

capital as opening "your love bank account" instead of just networking—success comes from first asking "what can I give?" It also offers guidance: What should you do when you hit a dry patch and have no work? Network (of course). Clean your desk: "You'll be surprised by how a clean, tidy desk will affect your productivity." Add skills: "You can never have too many skills. Maybe it's time to learn how to write code, market more effectively, or use Photoshop. The more skills you have, the more marketable you'll be." Evaluate your business model: "Have you been undercharging?" Want to grow as a freelancer? "Reinvent yourself," "productize your services," and "elevate your stature." If you don't like being a freelancer and are just doing it to eat, you should consider "finding the perfect full-time job."[34]

In the Freelancers Union model contingent work becomes desirable, a choice that offers freedom and autonomy. "Freelancers are changing the definition of success. It's no longer about the corner office in a soulless glass tower. It's about building and sharing real value together—investing in time, community, and well-being." The group sees this more "mindful approach to work" as a "pyramid of self-actualization." At the bottom of the pyramid are the stressed-out, struggling "unfree" freelancers, followed by the slightly better off, but probably still surviving on ramen (or the trust fund), "hustling" freelancers. Moving up past the "empowered" and the "influential" freelancers we reach the top: the

---

34   Ibid.; Freelancers Union, Instagram, February 18, 2014.

"360 degrees Freelancer." But the pinnacle isn't about money, status, or applause. "It's about giving back."[35]

The Freelancers Union is part of an emerging social movement called "new mutualism" that's grounded in the concept of a sharing economy. Jeremy Rifkin sees the sharing economy as the next big thing. He argues that hundreds of millions of people are already on board, sharing "information, entertainment, green energy, and 3D printed products at near-zero marginal cost." People are also sharing more personal things like clothes, homes, and household items.[36] "Flexible," "diversified" freelancers are the archetypal sharers:

> They mentor. They give without asking what they get. They see an opportunity and bring people together to seize it. But, most important, they're seeing beyond today. They know that the future will look very different than the present—and they're getting ready for it. Maybe they're part of a small cooperative of graphic designers who band together to help market each other and keep costs down. Or they make sure they buy from and work with other local freelancers to keep the ecosystem healthy. They buy their groceries at the local food co-op. They attend classes. They teach classes. They go to networking events not just to hand out business cards, but to find other freelancers that share their passions.[37]

---

35   Freelancersunion.org.
36   Jeremy Rifkin, "The Rise of the Sharing Economy," *Los Angeles Times*, April 6, 2014.
37   Freelancersunion.org.

In the new sharing economy we'll all be freelancers. We'll rent out our spare rooms on Airbnb and drive our cars for Lyft. We'll have a "portfolio of jobs" and live our lives by "essentialist" principles: We will live with "intention and choice" and celebrate the joy of "fulfilling a purpose" and making "small choices that lead to big change."[38]

It's all about adapting ourselves and acquiring the necessary skills and connections to make it in the world. This is the new American Dream. Sure, there are problems in society, but we don't need to change the world. We just need to change ourselves and the problems will disappear.

Reconsidering the American Dream

Renowned sociologist C. Wright Mills once said that "by the fact of [our] living [we] contribute, however minutely, to the shaping of this society and to the course of history, even as [we are] made by society and by its historical push and shove." The interplay of biography and history is central: To comprehend the possibilities for individuals we must look beyond their personal stories and milieus and situate them within the economic and political structures of the society they live in. One can "know their own chances in life only by becoming aware of those of all individuals in their circumstances."[39]

---

38   Ibid.; see also Atossa Araxia Abrahamian's piece on the Freelancers Union in *Dissent*, Winter 2012.

39   C. Wright Mills, *The Sociological Imagination*, New York: Oxford University Press, 2000 [1959], p. 6.

Oprah is appealing precisely because her stories hide the role of political, economic, and social structures. Instead of examining the interplay of biography and history, they eliminate it, making structure and agency indistinguishable. In doing so, they make the American Dream seem attainable. If we just fix ourselves, we can achieve our goals. For some people the American Dream is attainable, but to understand the chances for everyone, we need to look dispassionately at the factors that shape success.

The current incarnation of the American Dream narrative holds that if you acquire enough cultural capital (skills and education) and social capital (connections, access to networks) you will be able to translate that capital into both economic capital (cash money) and happiness. Cultural capital and social capital are seen as there for the taking (particularly with advances in internet technology), so the only additional necessary ingredients are pluck, passion, and persistence—all attributes that allegedly come from inside us.

The renowned French sociologist Pierre Bourdieu was very interested in the nature of capital. He saw the social world as a web of social relations whose dimensions were the result of "accumulated history," so that the social relations that constitute society do not appear and disappear spontaneously, nor are they random or equal. Instead, the social relations of society are shaped by power, and in particular, by the accumulation of capital. Bourdieu argued that capital accumulation

is what makes the games of society—not least, the economic game—something other than simple games of chance offering at every moment the possibility of a miracle. Roulette, which holds out the opportunity of winning a lot of money in a short space of time, and therefore of changing one's social status quasi-instantaneously, and in which the winnings of the previous spin of the wheel can be staked and lost at every new spin, gives a fairly accurate image of this imaginary universe of perfect competition or perfect equality of opportunity, a world without inertia, without accumulation, without heredity or acquired properties, in which every moment is perfectly independent of the previous one ... and every prize can be attained, instantaneously, by everyone, so that at each moment anyone can become anything.[40]

Bourdieu rejected this roulette image of social relations. He argued that the unequal ability of people from different socio-economic backgrounds to accumulate capital—economic, social, cultural—shapes their life chances profoundly and ensures that some will succeed while others will not. Though our society professes to be a competitive meritocracy—a "universe . . . of perfect opportunity, a world without inertia, without accumulation, without heredity, or acquired properties"—Bourdieu argued that, in nearly every instance, one's access to economic, cultural, and social capital determines success, not gumption and grit.

Social and cultural capital are forms of capital just like

---

40   Pierre Bourdieu, "The Forms of Capital," in J. Richardson, ed., *Handbook of Theory and Research for the Sociology of Education*, New York: Greenwood, 1986, pp. 241–58.

economic capital. They can be achieved as an end in themselves (for fun or edification or both), but their historical purpose has always been to protect wealth, help in the competition for wealth, and identify insiders (the rich) and outsiders (the riffraff). The American Dream is premised on the assumption that if you work hard economic opportunity will present itself and financial stability will follow, but the role of cultural and social capital in paving the road to wealth and fulfillment, or blocking it, may be just as important as economic capital. Some people are able to translate their skills, knowledge, and connections into economic opportunity and financial stability, and some are not—either because their skills, knowledge, and connections don't seem to work as well, or they can't acquire them in the first place because they're too poor.

Today, the centrality of social and cultural capital is obscured (sometimes deliberately), as demonstrated in the implicit and explicit message of Oprah and her ideological colleagues. In their stories, and many others like them, cultural and social capital are easy to acquire. They tell us to get an education. Too poor? Take an online course. Go to Khan Academy. They tell us to meet people, build up our network. Don't have any connected family members? Join LinkedIn. It's simple. Anyone can become anything. There's no distinction between the quality and productivity of different people's social and cultural capital. We're all building our skills. We're all networking. All types of social and cultural capital are equally translatable into economic capital (and happiness), and social and cultural capital will retain their value no matter how many people acquire them.

This is a fiction. If all or most forms of social and cultural capital were equally valuable and accessible—as the hegemonic narrative tells us they are—we should see the effects of this in increased upward mobility and wealth created anew by new people in each generation rather than passed down and expanded from one generation to the next. The data do not demonstrate this upward mobility. The United States, in a sample of thirteen wealthy countries, ranks highest on inequality and lowest on intergenerational earnings mobility.[41] Wealth isn't earned fresh in each new generation by plucky go-getters. It is passed down, preserved, and expanded through generous tax laws and the assiduous transmission of social and cultural capital.

Rich people's social and cultural capital is simply much more productive than the capital of the middle-class and working class. "Between 1979 and 2007 the top 1 percent of earners saw their after tax incomes rise 275 percent. The middle 60 percent saw their after-tax incomes rise 40 percent." Since the Great Recession the top 1 percent has grabbed 95 percent of the income gains. Rich people distinguish themselves and protect their wealth by using their power to reproduce themselves through massive investments in their children starting *in utero*. They use their social connections and wealth to write and pass legislation, open doors, navigate

---

41 Miles Corak, "Income Inequality, Equality of Opportunity, and Intergenerational Mobility," Discussion Paper No. 7520, Bonn: Forschungsinstitut zur Zukunft der Arbeit, July 2013.

the corridors of power, and provide an elite education and robust safety net for their children. The internet, social networking, and rags-to-riches stories don't change these facts. Going to State University and stalking potential employers on LinkedIn is not equivalent to going to Harvard and having a CEO for an uncle. As economist Thomas Picketty has shown, the rich are getting richer and will in all likelihood—given the current relationship between returns on capital and economic growth—get even richer.[42] The middle class is slipping and trying desperately to stick its foot in the closing door to wealth and power. But as more and more people compete to acquire the same social and cultural capital, the more each person needs ever greater amounts of social and cultural capital, and the less that social and cultural capital is worth.

The mind-cure stories that people like Oprah tell us say this isn't the case. Social and cultural capital are there for the taking if we want them and try for them. The real barriers are inside us, so we should focus on the inside stuff, be grateful for adversity, give back, and, most important, learn to think differently about the world so we can seize the opportunities waiting for us. But in a system stacked against everyone but the wealthiest, the inside stuff is often all we are left with.

Jennifer Silva, a sociologist at Harvard, studies working-class youth and their coming-of-age experiences. Working-class youth today are cut off from the markers of adulthood expected by their parent's generation. Most of them will

42   Thomas Picketty, *Capital in the Twenty-First Century*, Cambridge, MA: Belknap Press, 2014.

never enjoy the traditional rites of passage (house, steady job, family) essential to the American Dream. Silva finds that, nonetheless, they have internalized the therapeutic, self-actualization, inside-stuff narrative, just like their middle-class counterparts. The narrative helps them deal with their shattered dreams and "ascribe meaning and order to the flux and uncertainty of their lives." However, "this alternative, therapeutic coming of age story ends not with marriage, home ownership, and a career, but with self-realization gleaned from denouncing a painful past and reconstructing an independent complete self."[43]

It is from this vantage point that we can also understand the anger at gatherings like Occupy Wall Street. Occupy comprised primarily young, middle-class twenty-somethings who have done nothing but passionately pursue social and cultural capital in the hopes of landing their dream job, but who have little to show for it except a mountain of student loan debt and a job at Banana Republic.[44] Opportunities for economic advancement aren't unlimited and open to all. They are strictly regulated and open to a (relative) few, mainly the wealthy, and as wealth becomes more concentrated economic opportunities contract.

The way we are told to get through it all and realize our dreams is always to adapt ourselves to the changing world,

---

43   Jennifer Silva, "Becoming a Neoliberal Subject: Working-Class Selfhood in an Age of Uncertainty," 2011, blogs.sciences-po.fr; Silva, "Constructing Adulthood in an Age of Uncertainty."
44   Ruth Milkman, Stephanie Luce, and Penny Lewis, "Changing the Subject: A Bottom-up Account of Occupy Wall Street," Murphy Institute, City University of New York, 2013.

not to change the world we live in. We demand little or nothing from the system, from the collective apparatus of powerful people and institutions. We only make demands of
ourselves. We are the perfect, depoliticized, complacent
neoliberal subjects.

And yet we're not. The popularity of mind-cure, inside-
stuff strategies for alleviating alienation and achieving autonomy and success rests on our deep, collective desire for meaning and creativity in the face of overwhelming structural
odds against achieving self-actualization. Literary critic and
political theorist Fredric Jameson would say that the Oprah
stories, and others like them, are able to "manage our desires"
only because they appeal to deep fantasies about how we
want to live our lives. This, after all, is what the American
Dream narrative is about—not necessarily a description of
life lived, but a vision of how life should be lived. When the
stories that manage our desires break their promises over and
over, the stories themselves become fuel for change and open
a space for new, radical stories. These new stories must
feature collective demands that provide a critical perspective
on the real limits to success in our society and foster a vision
of life that does fulfill the desire for self-actualization.[45]

---

45   Fredric Jameson, "Reification and Utopia in Mass Culture," *Social
Text* 1 (Winter 1979), 130–48. See Kathi Weeks in *The Problem with Work* on
the power of the demand.

4
The Gates Foundation and the
Rise of Philanthrocapitalism

"Never doubt that a small group of thoughtful, committed citizens can change the world. Indeed, it is the only thing that ever has." Cultural anthropologist Margaret Mead may or may not have said this, but it is Melinda Gates's favorite quote, and it aptly sums up the philosophy of the Bill and Melinda Gates Foundation. The Gateses *are* changing the world. Since its founding in 1997, the Gates Foundation has transformed the medical and research fields for diseases like malaria and pneumonia and is at the center of an education reform movement in the United States. The Gates's recent efforts to publicize philanthropy, and their ability to leverage their wealth for social change, are encouraging other billionaires to commit to the Giving Pledge to donate the majority of their wealth to charitable causes.

The transformation of Bill Gates's image over the past two decades is remarkable. Gates, the ruthless, greedy monopolist, caricatured by Tim Robbins in the 2001 film *Antitrust*, has been supplanted by the earnest, humble Bill, a "worldwide force for good."[1] Melinda Gates, the other half of the foundation, is a shyer Samaritan, but is equally influential in shaping the foundation's trajectory. *Forbes* ranks her at number three on its 2014 list of the World's Most Powerful Women, right behind Angela Merkel and Janet Yellen.

The Gates Foundation is at the forefront of a new form of philanthropy called "philanthrocapitalism." Unlike the traditional foundations (Rockefeller, Carnegie, Ford), philanthrocapitalists don't believe in old-fashioned charity. They have greater ambitions. Philanthrocapitalists want to harness the forces of capitalism that made them fabulously wealthy to help out the rest of the planet. As Bill Gates said in his Harvard commencement speech in 2007, "If we can find approaches that meet the needs of the poor in ways that generate profits for business and votes for politicians, we will have found a sustainable way to reduce inequity in the world."[2] Philanthrocapitalists think profitable solutions to social problems are superior to unprofitable ones because they give private capital an incentive to care.

These new philanthropists are no less popular for their devotion to profit. In an era of declining state legitimacy and yawning social divides, people and countries are looking for solutions, and the philanthrocapitalists seem to have them. Matthew Bishop, New York bureau chief for the *Economist*, and Michael Green, a writer and economist, call philanthropists like the Gates "hyperagents"—actors "who have the

---

1   Randall Smith, "As His Foundation Has Grown, Gates Has Slowed His Donations," *New York Times*, May 26, 2014.

2   Bill Gates, Harvard commencement speech, June 7, 2007.

capacity to do some essential things far better than anyone else" because they don't have to deal with voters, shareholder demands, or fundraising. They are free to think outside the box and take risks.[3]

The source of these hyperagents' superpowers is the mountains of money they have made over the past three decades. Dramatic political, economic, and social changes since the late 1970s resulting in the rise of finance, sharp declines in taxes on wealth, the tech boom, and globalization have created windfall gains for people like the Gateses, the Waltons, the Broads, and the Buffets, to name only a few. But, as some of these billionaires have acknowledged, the world has not benefited equally. Absolute poverty and childhood mortality are declining in many countries, but starvation and chronic hunger afflict more than a billion people. Every year millions of children die from preventable diseases and a third of the planet lacks clean water and access to a toilet. When Bill Gates came up for air in the late 1990s after creating the Microsoft empire he looked around and was "shocked" and "revolted" by the fate of poor people around the world. "We had just assumed that if millions of children were dying and they could be saved, the world would make it a priority to discover and deliver the medicines to save them. But it did not."[4] Instead, he saw a system in which capitalist markets create health and prosperity for some but death and disease for others.

Rather than throwing up their hands in despair, the Gateses

3 Matthew Bishop and Michael Green, *Philanthrocapitalism: How the Rich Can Save the World*, New York: Bloomsbury Press, 2008, p.12.
4 Bill Gates, Harvard commencement speech.

decided to channel their business acumen, penchant for innovation, and money into "refining the system."[5] As successful businesspeople, the Gateses have a deep appreciation of the power of markets and view the problems of poor people as primarily a result of market inefficiencies. They note that while capitalist markets are great at creating wealth and spurring innovation, they don't naturally create equality. At the same time, governments and the private sector don't naturally put their resources into the right places to fix problems caused by market inefficiencies.

To ameliorate market inefficiencies, the Gateses set up a foundation with the resources necessary to change market incentives and rechannel "economic signals." Their donations, along with Warren Buffet's annual contribution of about $2 billion, have created a foundation with an endowment of more than $40 billion, triple the size of the Ford Foundation, the next-largest foundation. Having this much money enables the foundation to "make bets on promising solutions that governments and businesses can't afford to make."[6]

These bets are risky and sometimes fail, but the Gateses say that their projects are always guided by a simple principle: every life has equal value. As Melinda Gates says: "We don't think that everybody has the same chance to grow up and live a healthy life and yet we think they ought to have that. We think there's something that our foundation can do

---

5   Bill Gates, "A New Approach to Capitalism in the 21st Century," speech at the World Economic Forum 2008, Davos, Switzerland, January 24, 2008.

6   See www.gatesfoundation.org.

about that . . ."[7] Bill Gates told the graduating class of Harvard that "humanity's greatest advances are not in its discoveries but in how those discoveries are applied to reduce inequity. Whether through democracy, strong public education, quality health care, or broad economic opportunity—reducing inequity is the highest human achievement."[8]

In a world characterized by an unprecedented divide between rich and poor, this might sound daunting. But the Gateses are optimists. In their 2014 annual letter, they say that "[b]y almost any measure, the world is better than it has ever been."[9] They believe that people ·are beginning to recognize the need to tackle social problems and that for the first time in history we have the tools—biotech, computers, the internet—to make lasting social change.

NGOs, Foundations, and Civil Society

Nongovernmental organizations (NGOs) have been an important part of American civic life since the nineteenth century. Their numbers have waxed and waned, but beginning in the post–World War II era, many countries, including the United States, saw a huge increase in the number of NGOs. The spread of internet technology in the 1990s gave NGOs an international presence and helped to solidify their power and influence.

7　Melinda Gates, Entrepreneurial Thought Leaders Seminar, Stanford Center for Professional Development, November 14, 2012.

8　Bill Gates, Harvard commencement speech.

9　2014 Gates Annual Letter, http://annualletter.gatesfoundation.org/.

The growing importance of international NGOs (INGOs) is a story intimately linked to the economic and political changes resulting from the collapse of the Bretton Woods system in the 1970s and the 1980s debt crisis. As rural sociologist Phil McMichael argues, in the 1980s the "development project"—in which poor countries implemented national development strategies geared toward economic self-sufficiency and political sovereignty—was replaced by the "globalization project"—an ideological turn that encouraged states to lower their trade barriers, privatize resources and services, and embed themselves in global value chains.[10] In this climate, national states lost legitimacy and, during the debt crisis, structural adjustment programs forced developing countries to dramatically curtail spending on health, education, and food subsidies. To ameliorate the human crisis that resulted, international governing bodies (UN, IMF, World Bank) encouraged poor states to outsource welfare provision to Western INGOs, which were considered more efficient and knowledgeable than local institutions. Today, NGOs are a central part of global governance networks. They carry out aid work, conduct research, write policy reports, serve as experts, and act as conduits for development aid.

International NGOs are able to carry out these tasks because many of them are extremely well funded. Amnesty International, for example, has a bigger annual budget ($295 million in 2012) than the UN Human Rights Council ($177 million in 2012/13).[11]

---

10   Phillip McMichael, *Development and Social Change: A Global Perspective*, Newbury Park, CA: Pine Forge Press, 2008.
11   See http://files.amnesty.org/INGO/INGOAC.pdf.

Big INGOs, like Médecins Sans Frontières and Oxfam, receive public monies for many of their activities, such as fighting global poverty and providing humanitarian aid. But most NGOs rely on sympathetic individuals and money from large philanthropic foundations to fund their organizations.

Foundations, like NGOs, have historically played an important role in capitalism. Bishop and Green think we are actually in the midst of a *fifth* golden age of philanthropy:

> Since the birth of modern capitalism in Europe during the Middle Ages, rich businesspeople have consistently played a leading role in solving the big social problems of their day, often adapting the innovations of capitalism to make their philanthropy more effective. Indeed, to go further, it seems to be a feature of capitalism that golden ages of wealth creation give rise to golden ages of giving.[12]

Philanthropy booms, triggered by rapid increases in inequality during periods of massive wealth expansion, serve as a kind of release valve for capitalism by ameliorating some of its worst excesses. Joan Roelofs, a political scientist and expert on the (former) giants of the foundation world (Rockefeller, Carnegie, Ford), notes that the tycoons of the early twentieth century sought to "dole out their benevolence in a systematic manner. They also hoped to extract influence over social progress and public opinion, which was intensely anti-capitalist at the time" by working behind the scenes to shape movements and policy.

12   Bishop and Green, *Philanthrocapitalism*, p. 21.

The National Association for the Advancement of Colored People (NAACP), founded in 1909, was funded with money from numerous foundations, including Rosenwald, Peabody, and Rockefeller, and served as a crucial counterweight to the growing appeal of the Communist Party for black Americans during the 1920s. New Deal legislation of the 1930s was written by the Social Science Research Council, a Rockefeller organization, while Lyndon Johnson's Great Society programs were developed from the Ford Foundation's "Gray Areas" experiments—urban renewal programs designed to curb urban unrest and political organizing.[13]

The story today is similar. The consequences of skyrocketing inequality are of increasing concern, particularly to the super-elites. They worry about the long-term economic impacts of inequality, in terms of growth and innovation, and the political consequences of inequality—social unrest and demands for redistribution, particularly from the middle and upper-middle classes who believe in meritocracy. Philanthropy and public/private partnerships are once again being touted as ways to manage those risks and solve social problems.

Creative Capitalism

One can never be sure why someone goes to the trouble of making billions of dollars only to turn around and give them

---

13   Joan Roelofs, "Foundations and Collaboration," *Critical Sociology* 33: 3, May 2007, 479–504; see also G. William Domhoff, "The Ford Foundation in the Inner City: Forging and Alliance with Neighborhood Activists," www2.ucsc.edu/whorulesamerica/local/ford_foundation.html.

away. Some say it's the tax breaks, or perhaps a sense of civic duty. Others take a more ideological approach and argue that wealthy people want to decide what gets done with their money rather than leave it up to the state. Why Bill Gates decided to give his money away is anybody's guess. David Banks calls Gates's contributions "the antitrust dividend," noting that while Gates had given a few hundred million dollars to charity before 1998, his contributions in 1999 and 2000—the years of the federal antitrust trial against Microsoft—were staggering. Between October 1998 and January 2000 Gates put more than $20 billion into the foundation. Gates told an interviewer at the time that "he would gladly give up his fortune to make the antitrust trouble go away."[14] Gates himself says that he always planned to give his money away after he retired from Microsoft, but that his mother's persistent urging to give back pushed him to speed up his philanthropic aims following her death after a long battle with breast cancer in 1994.

Regardless of their motives, when it came time to choose *what* to spend their money on, Bill and Melinda followed their gut. Travelling around Africa in the 1990s, the Gateses were horrified by the fates of poor people, particularly children. They were also distressed that US students seem to be falling behind their international peers, and in particular, that poor students of color weren't getting the skills they needed to succeed in the new technology society. They asked themselves why, in an era of global abundance, were children dying or failing to reach their potential?

14   David Bank, *Breaking Windows: How Bill Gates Fumbled the Future of Microsoft*, New York: Free Press, 2001.

For Bill and Melinda Gates, the answer to both questions is inefficiencies in capitalist markets. "In a system of capitalism, as people's wealth rises, the financial incentive to serve them rises. As their wealth falls, the financial incentive to serve them falls, until it becomes zero," Gates remarked at the World Economic Forum in 2008. "Why do people benefit in inverse proportion to their need? Well, market incentives make that happen."[15] Even though poor people need more than wealthy people, there is no incentive to meet their needs because the needs are not coupled with the ability to pay. Thus, the Gateses contend that poor children are dying from disease and malnutrition, or not succeeding in school, because capitalist markets are not serving them.

The Gateses don't stop at identifying the problem. They have a solution: creative capitalism. They think businesses, NGOs, foundations, and governing organizations like national states and the UN, need to work together to "stretch the reach of market forces so that more people can make a profit, or gain recognition, doing work that eases the world's inequities." As Bill argues:

As I see it, there are two great forces of human nature: self-interest, and caring for others. Capitalism harnesses self-interest in a helpful and sustainable way, but only on behalf of those who can pay. Government aid and philanthropy channel our caring for those who can't pay. But to provide rapid improvement for the poor we need a system

---

15   Bill Gates, Davos speech, 2008.

that draws in innovators and businesses in a far better way than we do today.[16]

The Gates Foundation wants to lead the way in creating this better system by using its power to convert economic need into economic demand. To facilitate this transformation, the foundation spends billions of dollars annually in four program areas: Global Health, Global Development, US Programs, and Global Policy and Advocacy. Within these areas it has twenty-seven specific projects nested within a huge international network linking state actors, business, NGOs, and other foundations. The foundation's projects on vaccines and education demonstrate how creative capitalism works.

Vaccines

The Gates have gone in big on vaccines—so big that people avoid Bill at cocktail parties, afraid he'll drag them into a macabre conversation about tuberculosis.[17] In many low-income countries diseases such as malaria, rotavirus, and pneumonia remain killers. In the United States, these diseases are a spectre of times past: Swamp drainage, pesticide spraying, and massive sanitation infrastructure projects to supply clean water and safely dispose of waste have essentially eliminated these diseases from wealthy countries.

The foundation is pursuing a faster, potentially easier, route to eradicating disease in poor countries. The Gateses argue

16   Bill Gates, Davos speech, 2008.
17   Bishop and Green, *Philanthrocapitalism*.

that with advances in biotech and logistics we can develop vaccines for these diseases instead of getting tripped up on the bigger hurdles of providing clean water, sanitation infrastructure, and nutritious food. But the pharmaceuticals industry, concentrated in wealthy countries, has not developed such vaccines and is not particularly interested in doing so. As Bill Gates has wryly noted, they are more interested in cures for baldness than in cures for malaria. Why? Melinda Gates argues that there is simply no "rich world market" for products like diarrhea or pneumonia vaccines. Their solution is to use the Gates Foundation to create such a market in poor countries:

> [If] we could stimulate the pharmaceutical companies through public private partnerships to . . . create vaccines. If we could guarantee them a market of millions of children getting this vaccine and then being paid for it in the developing world. If we could commit to a market and we knew that the demand would be there, we could incent them with the right research dollars to actually create those vaccines.[18]

So how does this initiative work? First the foundation funds the research to develop the vaccines. It channels money into organizations like PATH, a Seattle-based group that runs the Malaria Vaccine Initiative and other groups like OneWorld Health, which works on antiparasite drugs. The foundation then tries to change the economic signals that guide market formation in developing countries. It does this by leveraging

---

18   Melinda Gates, Stanford seminar speech.

its money to put pressure on governments to buy vaccines for poor people, thus guaranteeing the market. Their deep pockets grease the wheels and convince governments and businesses to play along. (Even before Buffet's donation, the foundation had a bigger health budget than the World Health Organization.) The foundation also relies on other, smaller foundations like the Rockefeller Foundation and the David and Lucile Packard Foundation for institutional and logistical support. To date, the Gates Foundation has successfully brought both malaria and pneumonia vaccines to market. Through its Global Alliance for Vaccines and Immunization (GAVI), it has also vaccinated millions of children in the developing world against polio and other diseases.

Global health activism has a steep learning curve, but the Gateses are happy with the progress they have achieved. Global child mortality rates, despite the lost decade of the 1980s, have slowly, but steadily, declined since the 1970s. However, during the past two decades the declines have been much steeper. Total deaths of children under five dropped from 12.6 million in 1990 to 6.6 million in 2012. The annual rate of reduction between 2005 and 2012 was three times faster than between 1990 and 1995. The Gateses credit the foundation's efforts for the sharpening decline.

Education

The issue of education, while perhaps not as dire as childhood death from disease, is as close to the heart of the Gateses as any. Neither Bill nor Melinda Gates went to public school, but they argue passionately that the American school system is broken. Bill says that when he looked at the statistics for high school and college completion for US students he was "pretty stunned at how bad things are."[19] According to the National Center for Education Statistics, in the 2010/11 school year only 79 percent of high school students graduated on time. Minority, low-income, English-as-a-second-language speakers, and students with disabilities fell well below this national average. Over the past thirty years, a growing divide has emerged between those with a high school and those with a college degree. The earnings gap between high school and college graduates has doubled, while those without a high school degree can expect to earn a median annual income of $23,000 for their entire adult lives.[20]

The Gateses are not alone in decrying the failings of US public education. Thomas Friedman asserts that our public education system is "now outmoded for a flat world" and that "our love of television and video and online games" has made us complacent to the fact that other countries (China and India) are "racing us to the top"—and that we're losing.[21] A 2012 special taskforce, convened by the Council on Foreign Relations to assess the state of US primary and secondary

---

19   Bill Gates, "Mosquitos, Malaria, and Education," TED Talk, February 2009.
20   "Public High School Four-Year on-Time Graduation Rates and Event Dropout Rates: School Years 2010–11 and 2011–12," US Department of Education, NCES 2014–391; Lisa Dodson and Randy Albelda, "How Youth Are Put at Risk by Parents' Low-Wage Jobs," Center for Social Policy, University of Massachusetts, Boston, Fall 2012.
21   Thomas L. Friedman, *The World Is Flat: A Brief History of the Twenty-First Century*, New York: Picador, 2007.

education and its impact on national security, argued that "human capital will determine power in the current century, and the failure to produce that capital will undermine America's security . . . Large, undereducated swaths of the population damage the ability of the United States to physically defend itself, protect its secure information, conduct diplomacy, and grow its economy."[22]

Thus, it's not surprising that a quarter of all foundation money gets channeled into education reform. Hedge fund do-gooders started Democrats for Education Reform, and the Business Roundtable has its own Education Working Group. Billionaires like the Waltons, the Broads, and the Fishers have spent hundreds of millions on education reform, and the Gateses are at the center of it all. They argue that we need to completely re-envision public education if we are to prepare children for a high-tech future.

There are varying opinions on how to do it. Some, like the Waltons and the Broads, want school vouchers (government-issued certificates of funding that enable parents to send their children to private schools instead of public ones) and complete privatization. The Gateses think that vouchers have "some very positive characteristics" and praise the efficiency of parochial schools, but they think the public is too invested in public education and thus resistant to these kinds of sweeping change.[23] Instead, the Gates Foundation is pursuing

---

22 "US Education Reform and National Security," Independent Task Force Report No. 68, New York: Council on Foreign Relations, 2012.

23 Jason L. Riley, "Was the $5 Billion Worth It?" *Wall Street Journal*, July 23, 2011.

incremental change through the increased application of market mechanisms to public schooling.

The idea is that by applying a market logic to the public school system, educational entrepreneurs will want to get involved, creative people will get interested in education, and the resulting competition will force all schools to do a better job. As one reformer put it, by treating schools the same way we treat companies we can create a system where "every public school will have a performance contract where [the] people running it will have the freedom . . . to manage it well, hire and fire based on performance, [and] design their schools in a way that is successful . . . If they're not successful, they should be closed."[24]

The Race to the Top (RTTT) contest—President Obama's multibillion-dollar initiative to replace Bush's No Child Left Behind program—is a central part of this marketization strategy. The contest is designed to spur innovation, "scale-up entrepreneurial activity" and "encourage the creation of new markets for both for-profit and nonprofit investors" by forcing states to compete for education funding. Joane Weiss, former director of RTTT, says:

> The development of common standards and shared assessment radically alters the market for innovation in curriculum development, professional development, and formative assessments. Previously, these markets operated on a

---

24 Jim Horn and Ken Libby, "The Giving Business: Venture Philanthropy and the NewSchools Venture Fund," in Philip E. Kovacs, ed., *The Gates Foundation and the Future of US "Public" Schools*, New York: Routledge, 2011, pp. 172–3.

state-by-state basis, and often on a district-by-district basis.
But the adoption of common standards and shared assessments means that education entrepreneurs will enjoy
national markets where the best products can be taken to
scale.[25]

The best way to "scale-up" reforms and educational products is contested and prone to dead ends. The Gates Foundation
initially focused on reducing class size. In the early 2000s it
spent billions opening 2,600 small high schools in forty-five
states, but the project did not improve test scores, so it was
abandoned and many of the new schools were closed down.

Undeterred by this experience, the Gateses changed horses
and are now focused on teachers. The foundation argues that
some teachers are very effective at raising test scores, and that
these "top quartile" teachers are the key to improving student
performance, especially for disadvantaged students. The
Gateses believe that emphasizing poverty as a barrier to
educational attainment is empirically wrong and excuses bad
teaching. One in four US children might live in poverty, but as
Bill Gates told the National Urban League in 2011: "We know
that you can have a good school in a poor neighborhood, so
let's end the myth that we have to solve poverty before we
improve education. I say it's more the other way around:
improving education is the best way to solve poverty." As a

---

25   Diane Ravitch, *Reign of Error: The Hoax of the Privatization Movement
and the Danger to America's Public Schools*, New York: Knopf, 2013, pp.
16–17. Ravitch is an expert on public education and a fierce advocate for
students. In this chapter's discussion of education I draw heavily on her work
and encourage readers to visit her blog, dianeravitch.net.

bonus, if we keep only the good (top quartile) teachers, Bill thinks that "the entire difference between us and Asia would go away. Within four years we would be blowing everyone in the world away."[26] Powerful education reformers like Michelle Rhee, Joel Klein, Wendy Kopp, and Arne Duncan agree.

But according to the education reformers, there's a problem. Teachers are getting in the way of improving teaching. Anti-free-market mechanisms such as seniority, salary rewards for advanced degrees, and tenure are preventing real education reform. To weaken these barriers the foundation has funded new organizations like Teach Plus, started in 2009, and Educators 4 Excellence, founded by Teach for America alums Evan Stone and Sydney Morris in 2010. These groups bring young teachers to Washington to lobby against tenure and seniority rights. The foundation funded the development of Common Core State Standards (adopted by most states in 2010), a set of national standards that states must adopt and meet if they want Race to the Top funding. In conjunction with this initiative, the foundation is spending hundreds of millions of dollars on developing systems to measure teacher effectiveness. One of its projects videotapes the lessons of elementary school teachers. Over 13,000 lessons have been taped so far, enabling administrators and reformers to gauge what "effective" and "ineffective" teachers are doing in the classroom so they can replicate and scale-up effective teaching methods and weed out ineffective teachers.[27]

---

26   Ravitch, *Reign of Error*; Bill Gates, TED Talk.
27   Kovacs, *The Gates Foundation and the Future of US "Public" Schools*, pp. 172–3; Riley, "Was the $5 Billion Worth It?"

The Gateses certainly have the ear of power. Their vaccine initiatives are changing global health systems, and their US education projects are shaping federal education policy. But there are two central problems with the Gates model. First, it assumes that the key to solving thorny social problems is to deepen the reach of capitalist markets, despite the inequalities generated and reinforced by these markets. Second, the foundation's model to solve society's problems is profoundly undemocratic.

Using the Market to Do Good?

Capitalism and markets are not synonymous. When Bill and Melinda Gates talk about the power of markets, they mean profit-driven capitalist markets. As historian Fernand Braudel has shown, after the fifteenth-century capitalists slowly began to take over markets, altering the way they worked, and turning trade and production into activities geared toward the realization of profits rather than the satisfaction of human needs and desires.

Capitalist markets are not all bad. They can be liberating in many ways. Critical theorist Nancy Fraser argues they have enabled many women to gain the means to challenge and escape the repressive private sphere.[28] Capitalist markets spur technological and logistical innovation, and, of course, they generate unprecedented wealth.

---

28 Nancy Fraser, "Marketization, Social Protection, Emancipation: Toward a Neo-Polanyian Conception of Capitalist Crisis," in Calhoun and Derluguian, eds., *Business as Usual*.

The power of capitalist markets to do these things has encouraged a belief that all problems could be better solved by using a market logic. But what is market logic? In a capitalist market, the things we use and make are defined as commodities that are bought and sold on the market for a profit. In an optimal scenario, things that are of high quality and are efficiently produced are sold for a good price in the market and the capitalist makes a profit. The capitalist is happy with his profits, so he has an incentive to make more good things and to improve efficiency so he can make even more profits. Other capitalists want in on the game, so they compete to efficiently produce better or different things. We measure how well capitalists play the game by how much profit they make, and the unexamined assumption is that competition is the best way to allocate resources.

In this ideal scenario, everyone benefits when capitalists compete with each other to create the best things efficiently. In their competition to make profits capitalists constantly think up innovations that improve our lives. So the more things that get pulled into the market system and turned into commodities the better for everyone, because once a thing has the potential to generate a profit, incentives emerge for innovators to make that thing better and better.

Despite the purported benefits of transforming things into commodities, humans often resist this process. Episodes like the Diggers fighting against the enclosure of common land in Britain during the mid seventeenth century demonstrate how fraught the historical process of commodification has been. The Diggers were communities of farmers who believed that the earth represents a "common treasury" for all to share. They protested the loss of communal farming rights by building homes and planting food crops on common and waste lands across the English countryside. Wealthy landowners disapproved and called in the local gentry to burn down the Diggers' homes and destroy their crops.

The point of contention, whether 350 years ago or today, is that turning something into a commodity means it is no longer a right, or even potentially a right. It also means that the commodity's value is now judged primarily on whether it will turn a profit, and people's access to the commodity hinges upon their ability to pay for it.

The issue of vaccines is illustrative. The Gateses say that the problem with poor countries is that they are excluded from circuits of commodity production because they have no money and so generate no demand for things like vaccines. So the foundation supplies the demand for the pharmaceutical companies, giving the companies the incentive to supply the vaccines. In doing so, health care becomes a commodity with the hope that in the long run the foundation won't have to prop up the demand side and people will be able to buy the vaccines themselves. The problem is defined as a lack of commoditization, and the solution is to create a capitalist health care market. But should health care be a commodity that people buy and sell in the market?

In a wealthy country like the United States, where health care is a commodity, people buy the things they need (like visits to the doctor and medicine) to keep them healthy, and the state steps in and buys certain things (like vaccines) for people who can't buy them. But in a capitalist market, one's ability to purchase a commodity always depends on how much money one has. The US government does not want a public health crisis, so it makes sure people have vaccines and safe drinking water, but as scholars like Vincente Navarro have shown, beyond these basic levels access to care is highly stratified by class and race.[29] People with money and good health insurance live significantly longer than poor people with no health insurance. The difference in life span between a poor black man and a wealthy white woman is more than fourteen years. Despite being the wealthiest country in the world, the United States ranks 46th in infant mortality behind every rich country and even much poorer countries such as South Korea and Cuba. Babies born in poor states like Alabama and Mississippi are more than twice as likely to die before their first birthday than babies born in wealthy states like Massachusetts. The capitalist market creates winners and losers. When health care is a commodity, people die (45,000 preventable deaths per year in the United States) or suffer from chronic ailments because they don't have health insurance.[30] The Affordable Care Act, passed in 2010, is designed to close some of these gaps by expanding the number of people who can purchase

29   Vicente Navarro, "Race or Class versus Race and Class: Mortality Differentials in the United States," *Lancet* 336: 8725, 1990: 1238–40.
30   Sarah C. P. Williams, "Gone Too Soon: What's Behind the High Infant Mortality Rate," *Stanford Medicine*, Fall 2013; David Cecere, "New Study Finds 45,000 Deaths Annually Linked to Lack of Health Insurance," *Harvard Gazette*, September 17, 2009.

health insurance, but it stops far short of making health care a right.

Anything and everything should be done to save people's lives because no one should die from preventable diseases. But when we frame the problem of poor people in the Global South dying from preventable diseases as a market failure problem, we close off the possibility of building a health care system in which health care is a right and does not depend on one's ability to pay.

There is a growing global consensus on the importance of providing universal health care, as demonstrated by a 2014 World Bank event called Toward Universal Health Coverage by 2030. Margaret Chan, director-general of the World Health Organization, proclaimed that "we will not end poverty without universal health coverage." World Bank President Jim Yong Kim and Larry Summers, economist and former director of the US National Economic Council, echoed these sentiments. The Gateses do not agree. The foundation's official position is that it has no position on universal health care. Despite a report (which the foundation funded) published in *The Lancet* calling for universal health coverage, the foundation's Post-2015 Development Report states that universal health coverage has "limitations as a global development goal," and that evidence for its positive effects on health outcomes is "mixed."[31]

---

31   Tom Paulson, "Gates Foundation Won't Take a Stand on Universal Health Coverage," *Humanosphere*, April 15, 2014; Carol Welch and Clint Pecenka, "Health in the Post-2015 Development Agenda," Seattle: Bill and Melinda Gates Foundation, 2013.

The foundation's deep pockets give it an enormous amount of leverage to shape the way people think about health care globally. The Gates's position that health care works best as a commodity, despite overwhelming evidence that countries with universal health care have the best health outcomes, is deeply problematic and closes the door to frameworks that consider the underlying causes of global health disparities.

The Gateses also think that market logic should apply to public education. Bill Gates argues that the "top-down government monopoly provider" system is broken and that public education would be vastly improved with more competition.[32] The Gateses aren't advocating for a complete privatization of the US education system, unlike some other education reformers. Instead, they argue that public schools should operate according to a market logic, meaning that they should have to compete with other schools and demonstrate their value through improved test scores or else be shut down and/or replaced with private, charter schools.

According to Bill Gates, public education in the United States is failing because we don't hold teachers to the same standards as we do other professionals:

> The value of measuring effectiveness is clear when you compare teachers to members of other professions— farmers, engineers, computer programmers, even athletes. These professionals are more advanced . . . because they have clear indicators of excellence, their success depends

32 Riley, "Was the $5 Billion Worth It?"

on performance and they eagerly learn from the best. The same advances haven't been made in teaching because we haven't built a system to measure and promote excellence.[33]

The market logic is straightforward. The product of education (test scores) will be improved when educational production processes (teachers) transform the inputs (students) with more skill and efficiency. Right now the state has a monopoly on education, so we aren't able to optimize production processes by getting rid of teachers who aren't effective at producing high scores. Programs like Race to the Top and the (Gates-funded) Common Core state standards will enable us to optimize our production processes by increasing the frequency and number of standardized tests so that we'll be able to accurately measure the value each teacher adds to her students.

But there is a problem with applying capitalist market logic to education. The way a capitalist makes money is by using the best inputs and the most efficient production processes to make the most profits. This logic can't be applied to schools. Why? Jamie Vollmer, a businessman who once thought education should be run like a business, explains it well: In 1991, in the thick of the lean-production, "total quality management" craze inspired by the breakout success of Japanese manufacturers, Vollmer was lecturing a group of teachers, administrators, and staff on how to improve their

33   Bill Gates, "How Teacher Development Could Revolutionize Our Schools," *Washington Post*, February 28, 2011.

school. Vollmer ran a highly successful ice cream company whose blueberry ice cream had been voted America's best in 1984. He told the group that they should run their school like he ran his company.

During the Q&A a teacher stood up and asked him how he made such delicious blueberry ice cream. He informed her that he only used "super-premium" ingredients. She then asked him, "Mr. Vollmer, when you are standing on your receiving dock and you see an inferior shipment of blueberries arrive, what do you do?" He replied, "I send them back." The teacher jumped to her feet. "That's right!" But "we can never send back our blueberries. We take them big, small, rich, poor, gifted, exceptional, abused, frightened, confident, homeless, rude, and brilliant. We take them with ADHD, junior rheumatoid arthritis, and English as their second language. We take them all! Every one! And that, Mr. Vollmer, is why it's not a business. It's school!" All 290 teachers, principals, bus drivers, aides, custodians, and secretaries jumped to their feet and yelled, "Yeah! Blueberries! Blueberries!"[34]

Vollmer realized then that children are not inputs, but today's reformers aren't there yet, as demonstrated by their enthusiasm for schools like the Knowledge Is Power Program (KIPP) chain of charter schools. According to Bill Gates, "There are a few places—very few—where great teachers are being made. A good example of one is a set of charter schools called KIPP."[35] The schools (which are funded by

34   A longer version of this vignette is available at www.jamievollmer. com/blueberries.
35   Bill Gates, TED Talk, 2009.

the Gateses) were founded by two Teach for America alums and cater to poor black and Latino students from urban neighborhoods. The KIPP schools follow an extended-day, strict disciplinary regime. Students learn how to walk, get off the bus, and use the restroom in the KIPP way. Students are not allowed to talk at school except to answer questions, and they have to "earn" their desks. At some KIPP schools students who break minor rules are isolated and forced to wear signs around their necks that read MISCREANT or CRETIN.

KIPP is not unique. At the Achievement First network of schools, minor infractions such as whispering, humming, or not following directions quickly enough, warrant "re-orientation"—students (including kindergartners) must wear a white pinny over their uniform shirt and are not allowed to speak with other students or participate in music or phys ed while wearing the pinny. To remove it the student must present an official apology to the class and get all of her teachers to sign a letter saying she is ready to be readmitted to the group, and her classmates must vote to decide whether to welcome her back to regular activities.[36]

Reformers say these disciplinary models (KIPP's is based on the work of Martin Seligman, an American psychologist whose techniques of "learned helplessness" have been adopted by the CIA to enhance torture) are worth it because they dramatically improve test scores. What they do not say is that students who cannot conform are "counseled out" or

---

36 Kathleen Megan, "Charter School Group Gears Up to Lower Suspension Rate," *Hartford Courant*, July 8, 2013.

expelled. Only 40 percent of students who start at KIPP schools finish.[37] At a Hartford, Connecticut, Achievement First school nearly half the school was suspended during the 2011/12 school year, including kindergartners. Low-performing students and students with psychological or emotional disabilities are also less likely to be admitted to charter schools in the first place, and more likely to be suspended or expelled. This practice is so widespread among charter schools that the US Department of Education issued a "guidance" to charter schools in 2014 reminding them that they must comply with federal civil rights laws.

No one would claim that the purpose of education is to produce high test scores, or students who nod in unison, spend hours in complete silence, and be humiliated and debased for minor infractions. Yet this is precisely what happens when we organize schools according to a market logic. Education is not a commodity, learning is not a production process, and children are not human capital.

Undemocratic and Unaccountable

The second, and perhaps even bigger, problem with foundations (and many NGOs) is that they are profoundly undemocratic. They can use their money to fund absolutely anything they want. Their deep pockets give them open access to the corridors of power, and they are completely unaccountable for any negative outcomes that may occur as a result of their programs.

---

37   Erik. W. Robelen, "KIPP Study Finds High Student Attrition amid Big Learning Gains," *Education Week*, September 24, 2008.

This may seem like an extreme indictment. After all, polio vaccines and bednets in malaria-ridden places are good things, as is challenging Malthusian narratives of population growth and promoting contraception, which the Gates Foundation also does. But the Gates Foundation does whatever it wants. The Alliance for a Green Revolution in Africa (AGRA), a Gates/Rockefeller joint project that started in 2006, is one such example. The foundation contends that since the vast majority of poor people in African countries like Tanzania, Mozambique, Mali, and Ghana are farmers, improving the productivity and yields of farmers will lay the foundation for more sustained economic growth and pull people out of poverty. The goal with AGRA, as with other Gates projects, is to show investors that there are profits to be made in African agriculture. To demonstrate this, AGRA is implementing programs to create input markets in Africa for seeds, pesticides, and new loan programs for farmers.

AGRA argues that one of the major barriers to success (measured by improved yields) for African farmers is that they rely on informal, shared-seed systems. AGRA's plan is to replace these shared seeds with hybrid, high-yield seeds and in the process demonstrate that there is money to be made improving African seeds. These new seeds will be supplied by new, local private seed retailers in formal seed markets and protected by intellectual property rights. The new "certified" seeds will require increased pesticide use, so the foundation is also supporting the creation of pesticide markets. (The Gates's ownership of 500,000 shares in Monsanto may partially explain their enthusiasm for genetically modified seeds.)

When AGRA was announced it sparked an outcry from scientists, development scholars, and food sovereignty activists from both the Global South and North.[38] They argue that the Green Revolution hasn't passed over Africa, as AGRA's title suggests. The World Bank tried for decades to implement Green Revolution programs in poor African countries, and these efforts not only failed, but left increased levels of inequality, landlessness, and ecological damage in their wake.[39] AGRA policies are more sophisticated than the 1980s World Bank policies, but they trot out the same traditional-modern dichotomy, in which traditional (read: Backward) African farming practices are to blame for African poverty and malnutrition—a claim that doesn't hold up to empirical scrutiny.[40] Thus, African farmers should follow the modern (read: Smart) practices of Western farmers to increase productivity and pull themselves out of poverty.[41]

AGRA is an ongoing program and has generated sustained criticism from activists and political leaders around the world. In October 2014, representatives from six African countries and more than a dozen US food sovereignty groups convened

---

38   Eric Holt-Giménez, Miguel A. Altieri, and Peter Rosset, "Ten Reasons Why the Rockefeller and the Bill and Melinda Gates Foundations' Alliance for Another Green Revolution Will Not Solve the Problems of Poverty and Hunger in Sub-Saharan Africa," Food First Policy Brief No. 12, San Francisco: Food First, 2006.

39   For a good discussion of the Green Revolution and its problems, see McMichael, *Development and Social Change*.

40   Holt-Giménez, Altieri, and Rosset, "Ten Reasons."

41   "Giving with One Hand and Taking with Two: A Critique of AGRA's African Agricultural Status Report 2013," Johannesburg: African Centre for Biosafety, 2013, www.acbio.org.za/images/stories/dmdocuments/AGRA-report-Nov2013.pdf.

the Africa–US Food Sovereignty Strategy Summit in Seattle. But the outcry against AGRA has had little impact, because the foundation has the resources to pursue any policy goals it wishes. It has used its money to gain support inside the UN and from numerous other foundations and private donors, and it is accountable to no one other than Bill and Melinda Gates. The Gateses play down their power by situating themselves within a global network of partners that includes farmers and community groups, but the farmers who would supposedly benefit from the program have almost no voice in it. Simon Mwamba of the East African Small-Scale Farmers' Federation analogizes the situation: "You come. You buy the land. You make a plan. You build a house. Now you ask me, what color do I want to paint the kitchen? This is not participation!"[42] Instead of asking farmers and community groups how the foundation could support and strengthen the existing farmer seed system, the Gateses propose to replace the system with a new private one in which production and distribution are guided by a profit motive.

This is not just about voice. The absence of democratic mechanisms means that farmers have no way to stop a potentially devastating program. "On the assumption that commercially successful systems equal food security and social well-being," AGRA is proposing that African farmers (most of whom are too poor to buy seeds at any price) buy and use genetically modified seeds, which they are not allowed to

---

42 See AGRA Watch, www.seattleglobaljustice.org/agra-watch/about-us/.

reuse or share, as they have done for thousands of years.[43] There are serious ecological and developmental dangers in monoculture farming, and agro-ecologists worry about the growing crisis in US and European farming models. All of these problems are brushed aside in the AGRA initiative. The right of countries and their populations to food sovereignty is ignored. People from the West are experts, and African farmers are thought to be too poor and oppressed to come up with solutions and strategies.

The example of education in the United States is much the same. The Gateses and other education reformers have decided that the public education system in this country is broken. They say this over and over. It's broken, and they will fix it. But public education is not broken.

Modern day education reformers justify their incursions into the public education system by arguing that student test scores are lackluster and that the persistent achievement gap between black and white students demonstrates that minority students in particular are failing. According to National Assessment for Education Statistics (NAEP) data, test scores in math and reading for *all* fourth, eighth, and twelfth graders have improved over the past few decades, in some cases dramatically. In fact, scores for disadvantaged, minority students have improved the most out of all groups, and most of this improvement occurred before the current testing craze. High school graduation rates are at an all-time high, and more students than ever are going to college. The

---

43   African Centre for Biosafety, "Giving with One Hand," p. 18.

black–white achievement gap has narrowed but not disappeared, largely because both black and white students' test scores are improving. If one controls for income, the black–white achievement gap narrows even more.[44]

Stratification by income is actually the most striking trend in recent years. The achievement gap between high- and low-income students is substantially higher than it was three decades ago. Education reformers argue that there are good schools in poor neighborhoods, but household income and parental education levels are a major factor in life chances and educational attainment. Low-income students are seven times more likely to drop out of high school than high-income students.

These facts and considerations are lost in the conversation, and education reformers have been remarkably successful in creating a new "crisis" in education. Over the past decade and a half education reformers have dumped hundreds of millions of dollars into a campaign to convince Americans that their public education system is broken. Eli Broad, a major funder of education reform, admits that "the goal of the 'Ed in 08' campaign [was] to create a sense of crisis among the American public, a Sputnik moment . . ." The American public has been whipped up, to be sure, with lots of help from the Gateses and their allies. Films like *Waiting for Superman* paint the public school system as a horrible, corrupt, broken mess. The film made the cover of *New York* magazine, became the centerpiece of a two-part Oprah special on failing schools,

---

44 Robert Rothstein, March 8, 2011, www.epi.org/publication/fact-challenged_policy/.

and was promoted by Bill Gates (who funded the film) in a cross-country speaking tour.[45]

Crises in American schools seem to be a recurring phenomenon. When the Soviets launched Sputnik, the first artificial satellite, in 1957, Americans were stunned. They quickly blamed US schools for turning out second-best math and science students. And at the peak of Japan-bashing in the 1980s, pundits blamed public schooling for the inability of Americans to compete with Asian manufacturing rivals. Historian Richard Hofstader shows that our inclination to blame schooling (and teachers and school boards) for things we don't like reaches all the way back to the 1820s. But as Diane Ravitch, education historian and former "No Child Left Behind" advocate, argues, when reformers wax nostalgic about the good old days of schooling, they actually refer to a time when schools were racially segregated "were not required to accept children with physical, mental, or emotional handicaps; when there were relatively few students who did not speak or read English; and when few graduated from high school and went to college."[46]

All this is not to say that US education shouldn't be improved, or radically re-envisioned, or that we shouldn't be concerned about the significant income and racial gaps in achievement. It is simply to say that the public education system in the United States is not broken. The public has bought the media story of education in crisis, but when people are asked to rank their own schools—the ones their kids go

45 Dana Goldstein, "Grading 'Waiting for Superman,'" *Nation*, October 11, 2010.
46 Ravitch, *Reign of Error*, p. 33.

to—more than three-quarters of parents say they love their schools and their teachers.[47] The Chicago Teacher's Union strike in 2012 had massive community support. After the radical Caucus of Rank and File Educators, led by Karen Lewis, won a run-off election to lead the Chicago Teachers Union in 2010, they built a new network of teachers, parents, and community members from the ground up to take a stand against concessionary demands and school closures. In September 2012, after failed negotiations with the city over enrichment programs and teacher layoffs, Lewis took the CTU out on strike for the first time in twenty-five years. The teachers, like many public sector unionists who go on strike, were vilified in the press, but with the support of their community network they stood their ground and won.

Groups of parents and community members in cities like Newark and Washington DC are also incensed about school reform, and in particular the things that Cory Booker and Michelle Rhee have done to their schools. People don't want Common Core standards. They don't want to close schools and fire teachers. They don't want vouchers and more testing. They don't want public money to be used to privatize education. They realize that the problem with schools is really a problem with the economy. They realize that teachers and schools are not to blame for the fact that one in four children in this country grows up in poverty. In May 2013, 1,500 parents convened in Albany, New York, to protest high-stakes testing.

47   William J. Bushaw, "The Seven Most Surprising Findings of the 2012 PDK/Gallup Poll on Public Schools," *Education Week* blog, August 23, 2012.

A year later, hundreds of Camden, New Jersey, high school students walked out to protest teacher layoffs, while thousands of parents around the country in states like California, Washington, and Colorado are boycotting standardized tests.

The response by parents, students, and communities is building, but they face an uphill battle, because despite their frustration and anger they have little say in the education reform process. The Gates Foundation is a private institution that is free to use its money as it sees fit. It's not just Bill and Medinda Gates. Education reformers lobby Congress to pass legislation written by the American Legislative Exchange Council, an organization of conservative legislators and business groups that writes sample legislation for political representatives to present to Congress and state legislatures. When Mark Zuckerberg decided to donate $100 million to "fix" the Newark Public School System, the foundation board established to decide how to use the money had only a single community member on it—(former) Mayor Cory Booker.[48] Foundations are not only unaccountable and undemocratic—they often also implement programs and structures that are undemocratic. One of the central goals pushed by education reformers is to eliminate elected school boards—as did former New York City mayor Michael Bloomberg in 2002—the only voice for parents and communities to speak up about school reform.

The restructuring of the economy over the past few decades, the slashing of income and capital gains taxes, and the elimination of estate taxes have given the super-elite more

48   Maggie Severns, "Whatever Happened to the $100 Million Mark Zuckerberg Gave to Newark Schools?" *Mother Jones*, March 28, 2013.

money than ever before. They are using this money to follow their dreams of changing the world. The American public is subsidizing their dreams, because every dollar these billionaires write off as philanthropic giving isn't added to the public revenue. All this money adds up. As political economist and policy expert Robert Reich notes, "The US government spends more on subsidizing charitable donations than it does on Temporary Aid to Needy Families."[49] But the dreams of these foundations are not our dreams. We don't have a say in shaping them. The foundations are unregulated and unaccountable. They set the agenda. There is no democratic process through which citizens get to decide what to do with the money. In the end, Melinda Gates is half-right. A few people are changing the world. But they are not the only ones who ever did. Big changes also come from people using democratic channels to advance radical programs for social change. Foundations don't redistribute wealth, but social movements demanding that public wealth be used for the public good do.

---

49 Robert Reich, "A Failure of Philanthropy," *Stanford Social Innovation Review*, Winter 2005.

5
Looking Forward

Capitalism both creates and destroys, and the past three decades have been no exception. Unprecedented generation of wealth, global integration, and technological innovation have been accompanied by a stratospheric rise in inequality, ever-expanding environmental destruction, and a loss of faith in capitalism as the best possible system. Faith has been replaced by fatalism—most people recognize the deep problems associated with capitalism but doubt the possibility of a better way of organizing society.

Despite their vast wealth and success, the new prophets of capital also recognize these problems, but they haven't lost faith in the possibilities of capitalism. They believe that the solutions to our problems lie in refining the existing political and economic system, expanding the reach of capitalist markets, submitting more and more aspects of our lives to a market logic, and channeling our struggles for a better life through corporations.

The solutions proposed by these new prophets are seductive and resonant. Most of us share the concerns of Sheryl Sandberg, John Mackey, Oprah Winfrey, and Bill and Melinda

Gates, and we long for simple, feasible ways to improve society. But the stories and solutions they offer will not end inequality, poverty, alienation, oppression, or environmental degradation. They will not resolve the contradictions of capitalism. Instead, their solutions strengthen existing social relations of power and profit-driven structures of accumulation, and they in fact bolster the very forces that create these negative outcomes in the first place. Paradoxically, they are doing so by voicing grievances against capitalism, forcing the people, institutions, and structures that undergird it to evolve and temporarily work through crises, propping up and strengthening the system for the long haul.

Does this mean that it is pointless to challenge capitalism? That all critiques of the status quo will be absorbed, displaced, or ignored? Capitalism can accommodate the powerful women, the eco-business practices, the essentialist principles, and fund vaccine projects without missing a beat. That is because these critiques and projects do not challenge the in-built drives of the production-for-profit system. But stories and ideas that truly challenge the for-profit architecture are not easy for the existing power structure to absorb, divert, or implement. Were they to be incorporated, they would change the system in fundamental ways, because they are irreconcilable with the status quo. These ideas lay the groundwork for thinking about a very different kind of society—one that is driven by the dictates of human need, not profit.

What would a radical, anticapitalist model look like? To begin with, the model won't be a single, unified narrative of change. It will be comprised of thousands of stories, all with their own unique visions for a better world. These alternative stories, though they aren't usually loud enough to be picked up by the corporate media, already exist and are being told by more and more people. As part of the Ear to the Ground Project, longtime organizers and activists NTanya Lee and Steve Williams traveled all around the United States interviewing organizers fighting to make the world better—a world where oppression and poverty have no place. They found a myriad of collective projects, some new and some old, run by dedicated activists and organizers.[1]

This collective vision consists of projects with different immediate goals and philosophies. Some groups fight for environmental justice, while others fight for immigrant rights. Some groups want to organize fast food workers into unions, while others want to get high-stakes testing out of their children's schools. Some groups fight against domestic violence, while others fight for the civil rights of ex-offenders and prisoners. The passions and goals of these groups are formed by the passions and goals of the people who fight in them.

All these projects and ideas are different, to be sure. But the really transformative ones have core features in common that set them apart from projects and ideas that don't go beyond merely refining the system.

The first feature setting them apart is their emphasis on democracy, both as a means and as an end. Moving from a profit-driven to a human needs–driven society requires that

---

1   NTanya Lee and Steve Williams, "More Than We Imagined: Activists' Assessments on the Moment and the Way Forward," Ear to the Ground Project, eartothegroundproject.org.

the institutions we participate in and the places we spend our time (schools, workplaces, communities) be transformed into places where participants have a real voice in how they're run and what their purpose is. The United States is formally a democracy, and most citizens enjoy rights that people in many other countries do not enjoy, but both political parties preach a nearly identical program that channels benefits to elites while demanding that poor and working class people in the United States and abroad shoulder the costs of neoliberal capitalism.

Real democracy is possible only if we apply it to other spheres of life, including the workplaces and institutions we depend on. Workplaces should be owned and managed as cooperatives—places where workers control the business, distribute its surplus equally among themselves, and make decisions about their work-lives democratically. Banks, financial institutions, and the internet (institutions that are now essential to all people and businesses) should be transformed into public utilities. Educational policies should reflect the collective decisions of parents, teachers, and administrators. These types of projects will require us to radically rethink, and broaden, our definition of democracy. This may be a daunting task, but it's worth remembering that the democratic rights that we do enjoy were not handed down from the state or given to us by business, but are rather the product of centuries of struggle from below. This struggle must be expanded beyond the formal trappings of the electoral system, because a collective vision is simply not possible without everyone's voice.

The second principle that the radical, anticapitalist projects share is de-commodification. The history of capitalism has been characterized by both the transformation of more and more aspects of people's lives into commodities and the reshaping of our expectations, values, and norms to align with the needs of business. A fundamental component of any transformative vision is the fight to take back our lives from capitalist markets—to say that things like our health, our desire to learn, and have a roof over our heads should not be subject to our ability to pay. These things should be a right, not a commodity. Every time something is transformed from a right into a commodity the power of the profit motive to dictate our lives is increased. Conversely, whenever our collective projects remove things from the sphere of capitalist markets, we weaken the grip that capital has over our lives. If people aren't worried about losing their home or having no health insurance for their kids, they will be much more willing to stand up to their bosses and fight for projects to increase democracy. Social movements have long fought to de-commodify aspects of our lives and have, for short periods of time, succeeded. But our biggest mistake has been to settle for means-tested benefits—social gains that benefit only certain sectors of the population based on factors like income or occupational status. These benefits foment ill will among those who don't qualify for them and are easy political targets. The contrast between the dismantling of the US welfare system in the 1990s and the resistance, despite repeated attacks, to the elimination of Social Security is illustrative: Historically, welfare programs were available only to the poorest (and most stigmatized) members of society, excluding working-class and lower-middle-class households struggling to get by. Conservative opponents of welfare exploited this disparity, stoking anger among those getting no support toward those receiving (meager) state support. In contrast, Social Security is a benefit enjoyed by nearly everyone: only 4 percent of the population is excluded from receiving Social Security benefits, and 87 percent of Americans want to preserve Social Security for future generations. Creating the space to radically de-commodify our lives will require that social gains such as free higher education, single-payer universal health care, and a minimum basic income be made available to everyone regardless of their income.

The immediate goals of projects and ideas that embrace the principles of democratization and de-commodification may vary, but their long-term goal is always to make people's everyday lives better. To achieve these goals, groups and projects must emphasize a final principle: redistribution. The top 20 percent of households control nearly 90 percent of all wealth in the United States, while the super-elite (the top 0.1 percent) control more than 20 percent of all wealth. People in power of course downplay inequality. They say that just because a few people are extravagantly wealthy doesn't mean the rest of us can't be rich as well. And it is not only people in power who say this. Americans cherish their belief in meritocracy. They believe that if you work hard your circumstances and wealth won't determine your chances of success. This may hold for a small sample of the population, but at a systemic level it is patently false. Extreme concentration of wealth, enabled by tax laws favoring the rich, inhibits democracy and de-commodification in a fundamental way, starving the public treasury and eliminating the means to provide a good life for everyone. Since wealth creation is a collective process, a wealth tax would provide a way for wealth to be shared collectively, while a robust public treasury could ensure that the rights of all people to housing, food, health, education, and a clean environment are met.

These three principles don't constitute a magic formula, nor will such ideas and projects change the system overnight. There are no shortcuts. But there is possibility. In this present moment, characterized by crisis, uncertainty, and anxiety a new spirit of capitalism is being formulated. So far, the loudest voices defining the contours of the new spirit are those of the super-elite. People with money and power are preaching a new spirit of capitalism that absorbs and displaces radical criticisms of the status quo. Sheryl Sandberg, John Mackey, Oprah Winfrey, Bill and Melinda Gates, and others like them are developing a new ideology for why capitalism is the only, and best, system possible.

This doesn't have to be the case. At the end of the day, for capitalism to function most of us must believe in the system and voluntarily devote our energies to it. But these existing beliefs and norms are not primordial or fixed. They can change and evolve. Collective projects and radical visions can foster new dreams and ideas and different beliefs and norms about how we should organize our lives and society. Instead of thinking about how to fix capitalism, we can start thinking about a different kind of society. We can imagine a world designed for the needs of people instead of profit, and we can get to work building it.

Further Reading

In this short book I have drawn on the work of many scholars, distilling their analyses and frameworks to make a straightforward argument. Inevitably, the essence of what makes these works great is lost in such a process, so any reader interested in the topics discussed should turn to the original source material. Below is a condensed list of works that inform the theoretical framework of the book.

On ideology, stories, and society

Luc Boltanski and Eva Chiapello's *The New Spirit of Capitalism* is a major source of inspiration for this book and a must-read for anyone interested in capitalism's remarkable adaptability and longevity. Their book builds on the foundational work of Max Weber, and asks how capitalism evolves in the face of critique. They focus mainly on neoliberal management practices in France, but I have expanded their framework to think about the role of critique, ideology, and adaptation at the level of society.

On the market and the state

Karl Polanyi's classic, *The Great Transformation* has shaped my, and many other people's, thinking about the relationship between the state and the market, and how states create, shape, and sustain capitalist markets. There is also a great deal more recent scholarship that deals with these questions. Greta Krippner unravels the relationship between the state and financial markets during the neoliberal era in her book, *Capitalizing on Crisis*. Bernard Harcourt approaches the question from a different angle in his examination of free market ideology and punishment in *The Illusion of Free Markets*. Sam Gindin and Leo Panitch use a wide-angle lens in their book *The Making of Global Capitalism* to show how the US state has played a central role in creating and sustaining global capitalism.

On nature

The relationship between nature and capitalism has been explored by many authors, though perhaps most fruitfully by Neil Smith in *Uneven Development*. Smith's work examines how capitalist society creates not only space, but also nature itself. Erik Swyngdeouw's work explores similar themes. His article "Impossible Sustainability and the Post-Political Condition," (appearing in David Gibbs and Rob Krueger's *The Sustainable Development Paradox*) is a must-read for anyone interested in understanding the problems with sustainable capitalism.

On capitalism and neoliberalism

The body of literature on both capitalism and neoliberalism is incredibly broad. David Harvey has thought deeply about the fundamental drives of capitalism. In this book I drew from *The Enigma of Capital* but he has written numerous other great books that cover similar territory. Giovanni Arrighi's analyses of global capitalism, financialization, power, and hegemony are essential to any study of restructuring over the past three decades (see for example *The Long Twentieth Century* and *Adam Smith in Beijing*). Studies of neoliberalism run the gamut from economy to culture. Janice Peck's book *The Age of Oprah* is a fascinating window into the culture of neoliberalism and the cult of the individual.

On gender, work, and identity

Kathi Weeks has written a fantastic book dealing with questions of work and feminism: *The Problem with Work*. This examines the centrality of the work ethic to the feminist project, but also takes on much bigger questions about developing alternatives to dominant work-centric visions of utopia and the power of radical demands to create space for a new utopian vision. Any reader interested in work and labor more specifically should turn to classics like Harry Braverman's, *Labor and Monopoly Capital*, Dan Clawson's *The Next Upsurge*, Rick Fantasia's *Cultures of Solidarity*, and Beverly Silver's brilliant, *Forces of Labor*.

Acknowledgments

Even for a short book like this many thanks are in order. Marcos Marino Beiras and Richard Dienst introduced me to political economy and critical theory. Giovanni Arrighi and Beverly Silver patiently elucidated the processes of capitalism, and many of their ideas have found their way here. As mentor and friend Sam Gindin has profoundly shaped my thinking about resisting capital. Japonica Brown-Saracino, Myka Tucker Abramson, and Emilio Sauri all read chapter drafts. Myka helped me hash out my arguments over many cups of coffee, and Emilio and I have spent countless hours debating commodification. Thanks go to Audrea Lim at Verso for her helpful suggestions on the manuscript, Bhaskar Sunkara for his support and enthusiasm, and Remeike Forbes for his lovely cover design. Last but not least, many thanks go to my friends and family—Ellen Whitt and Bryan Nelson for their dedication to justice, Indrani Chatterjee and Susana Domingo-Amestoy for their companionship, and my mother Joan Aschoff for her steadfast support. For Pankaj Mehta, my partner in life, my debts are too great to express in words. I dedicate this book to my daughters Ila and Simi whose passion, energy, and love fill me with hope.